JOURNEY TO PARADISE

JOURNEY TO PARADISE

A MEMOIR

SARAH JOLICOEUR

atmosphere press

CONTENTS

FOREWORD

I love to read. I'm not a reader of classic literature or someone who picks up the newest novel everyone is talking about. Nope. I'm the one who reads a variety of books and views, but within a not-too-broad range. I love books on relationships, self-improvement, happiness, and cultivating your best life. I am a junkie for biographies on anyone who has made a difference (which is pretty much everyone). I read the occasional fiction book and am usually reading two to three books simultaneously. Positive/Happiness/Affirmation books in the morning and then biography or fiction at night. I don't devote as much time as I would like to, and I think reading twenty books a year is an accomplishment. Throughout all the genres, my absolute favorite type of book is one written from the point of view of the author. I love hearing other people's personal journeys and picking out the lessons as I read along. That is what I hope to have written for you here. Through my experiences, I hope you learn a thing or two. You can take it or leave it, but I do hope you enjoy it.

There were some parts of this that were extremely painful to write. It took weeks sometimes just to get a couple of sentences down because I had to go back to memories that I would rather forget. I pulled up lots of happy memories as well, that was the easy part. I did have the wonderful opportunity to pause and reflect on where we have been, what should have broken me, saw things maybe I should have left broken, and have seen how I've grown as a human. I questioned how the man I am married to today is the same man from thirteen years ago. I love it all, just had to get through the pain one last time to hopefully help others thrive.

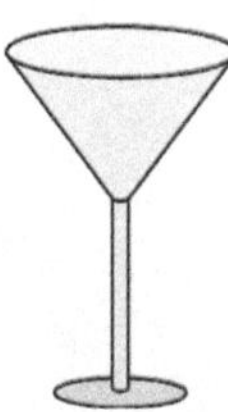

PART 1

CHAPTER 1

WHERE I BEGAN

"Each time of life has its own kind of love."
— Leo Tolstoy —

This is my story. This is the journey of how I learned a multitude of new words like: "lifestyle," open marriage, poly, and how I have learned to navigate my own marriage. Some of you might have just read that first sentence and thought, "Nope, I am none of those so this is definitely not for me" or "Ewww I would never" or "There's no way I could relate to your story, I could never do that." Here is the good news: I am a real woman, married to a real man, and we have the same struggles as every other married couple—we just structure our world a little differently. For sure there are some issues we have encountered monogamous couples can not relate to. But guess what, there are so many struggles we do have in common. We share different opinions on how the dishes should be put away and who will clean the house (Lovie is always the one to clean our house). It takes us hours to pick out a movie that I will inevitably fall asleep during. I like to go out to eat and he would rather cook at home. And then there are some others that we all have in common but that no one likes to admit out loud, like wanting to have sex with someone we aren't married to or thinking the random stranger who passed by is smoking hot or flirting with the bartender while on a business trip. Every relationship is unique and no matter what your lifestyle is, there will always be things no one else understands.

Never did I imagine I would be where I am in my relationship. Not with the man I am married to or on this path. I grew up with the picture-perfect family. Most people refer to my parents as June and Ward Cleaver. My dad was always the breadwinner and worked a typical 9-5 corporate job for most of my youth. My mom was a stay-at-home mom for most of what I remember, except for a couple of years when she worked at a mother's-day-out school when my baby sister was little.

I am the oldest of three girls meaning my dad was seriously outnumbered. Every day after school Mom had a snack ready on the kitchen table, nothing fancy, cheese and crackers or celery with peanut butter and raisins (she called it ants on a log) but looking back it was super special. I had friends who had to fend for themselves until late evening when their parents got off work, so being able to stroll through the door to a ready snack was a privilege. Every night Dad cooked dinner while watching the nightly news on a tiny black-and-white TV (at least I think it was black and white ...). This was in the late '90s and early 2000s, so this tiny screen with a huge back seemed like an ancient relic tucked in the corner between the stove and counter top. All five of us ate dinner together—every single night—there was always something green on the plate and milk to drink. Mom would be on cleanup duty. That was the routine.

There was a dreaded event that happened about every six months. We would get home from school and *everything* would be pulled from our closets, under the beds, and anywhere else we had stuff shoved and heaped in the middle of the floor—it was horrific. These were the times we wished Mom worked out of the house; none of our friends with working parents ever had to experience this. What's even worse, they made us clean it up ourselves. The nerve. Can you imagine kids today having to experience this? They would be triggered for sure. And to top it off, we were not allowed to go out with friends until it was cleaned up to their liking. No going outside for night games, no phone calls, no AOL chats, no cars, nothing. Luckily, my sisters and I picked up the lesson they were teaching us with this exercise: responsibility, cleanliness, and accountability for our own actions. They also taught us basic skills to take care of ourselves, how to do laundry, the value of money and, most importantly, showed us what a loving partnership marriage is.

My parents just celebrated their forty-second wedding anniversary. Not only are they still married, but they are still genuinely still in love. I can only remember one major disagreement ever in the eighteen years I lived at home and the only other times I can recall them raising their voices was during the occasional "budget review" (I can totally relate to that one). They have always fully supported each other. As an adult, I realize that there is no such thing as perfection and every couple has their things. However, they were pretty close to perfect from my view. I would be remiss not to mention that I come from a line of awesome examples. My mom's parents were married from 1956 until my grandfather passed away in 1993 from cancer. My dad's parents just celebrated their sixty-seventh anniversary and have worked their way through some incredibly tough times. I have been so blessed that I can call my grandma and ask for advice.

The relationship I have with my grandparents is still full of surprises of what life was like when they were my age—it is pretty crazy and awesome to hear. When they were first married, Pappas was in the service. In order for them to get married, he took a three-day leave; they got hitched, and he had to report back right away. Mammaw helped talk me through the different emotions she felt and how she handled the range of emotions that comes along with being a newlywed with two addresses. And while she has never had the same lifestyle, I can talk to her about anything I'm going through, and she has stories that I can apply to my situation, because the basis of life and love is fundamentally the same.

In high school, I did not date much. I had two or three boyfriends the entire four years, but nothing that was serious or involved many actual dates. Mostly it was boys at school whom I would hold hands with in the halls, eat lunch with, and talk on the phone with at night. I was the cool friend that the guys could talk to, and that worked for me. I had very little experience with boys coupled with a low self-esteem because I was so much bigger than my girlfriends. Let me clarify, by bigger, I mean D-cup, broad shoulders and hourglass figure. I was in no way fat. Just waaaay curvier than others. Oh ... and I had super bad acne, so there was that.

I lost my virginity thirteen days after turning fifteen. I considered us to be "dating." I'm 100 percent sure it was a one-sided opinion about that relationship. We were in the same church group and had attended different events and retreats together. When I say together, I mean in the same group, not actually as a couple. I had a huge crush on him, and he was a seventeen-year-old boy; he was not going to shove off my advances or miss an opportunity to make out. We never socialized except for church events or while skipping the teen program after church. Organized religion has never really been my thing, so it seemed like the perfect opportunity to sneak around with an older boy who did not go to my school. I only saw him once or twice a week.

He was a senior who was leaving for college, and I was about to start my sophomore year. On the night before he was leaving for Auburn University, we skipped church group with my best friend and his best friend, hopped in the car and drove around until we decided to park behind the empty movie theater. Naturally, he asked for his going-away gift to be sex; I do not actually know if it was his first time or not. But there, in the back seat of an Isuzu Rodeo, with my bestie and his best friend making out in the front seat, I lost my virginity. This might be seen as foreshadowing.

After high school graduation, I got my first apartment with a good friend. JR and I were in the same group of friends and had gotten close over the years. After everyone left for college, we got a two-bedroom, one-bath apartment together and were loving the free life. This little apartment kicked off our lives together and we've been lifelong best friends ever since. We have been through marriages, divorce, deaths, births, and every other imaginable life event together.

For the first time in my life, I was totally independently living in that tiny apartment. Okay, maybe not totally independent on my part—I still had a BP credit card (under Daddy's account) for gas that we may or may not have used to purchase groceries on occasion, and there was that one time I had to borrow money for rent because I got a tattoo instead. But still, no curfew. No parents to ground me if I was drinking underage. No rules. All we had to do was keep ourselves from getting arrested, find enough money for rent, and make sure we had food to eat.

Our neighbors in the small eight-unit building were amazing and loved to have a good time. We were the new chicks in the self-proclaimed party building, so we made friends immediately with all the single, twenty-something guys. There was a core group of six of us that started it all. JR and I on the top floor on the front side of the building. The Jock and his roommate, the Car Salesman, lived next door and upstairs so our patios were right next to each other. In order to go to the others' front door, you had to walk all the way down the stairs, across the front of the building into the parking lot, and up the other side of stairs. No one had time for that. So, we came up with a doorbell system: a Natural Light beer can. Yup, it was perfect. Anytime someone wanted to chat or needed something, they would just throw the beer can onto the patio. It was genius. On occasion, the beer-can doorbell was not good enough, so the Jock was somehow able to perform a spider monkey climb from his balcony onto ours and we would have unexpected company walking in our patio door.

Then there was the leasing agent–J—who lived directly underneath them. J was one of the first people to change the trajectory of my life. The top of the list was his influence in getting me onto my career path. He worked at the leasing office where JR and I lived. He was awful with paperwork and would pay us in resident referrals (meaning he would put our name on a person's application when they applied for an apartment, and we would get a check) to help him late at night. Once the manager found out what he was doing, she offered me a chance to interview. Thus started my career path in property management for the next twenty years. Every now and then, I think back to all the ways he helped me become who I am today and silently say thank you to him in my heart. He has always been the man to know. And he sure knew all the people. It was through him that we expanded our tribe in droves. It was one of the most eclectic groups ever put together. One night sitting in his apartment watching his new big screen (We were all between eighteen and twenty-four and bordering on broke so a TV that took up the entire wall was quite the entertainment.), there was a super cute country boy sporting a ball cap with a goatee with a huge burgundy, jacked-up truck sitting outside. I was smitten right away.

He thought I was cute, so J hooked us up and we dated for three blissful months. I felt so grown-up. He stayed the night in my bed, we went on actual dates to restaurants that he paid for, and I had someone to bring home to show off at Christmas. It was amazing while it lasted. When he ended it, I took the breakup hard, like devastating hard. Anyone other than JR would have assumed we had been together a long, long time based on how upset I was. That was probably because I had no experience in breaking up and had (okay, still have) a slight tendency to be dramatic. Luckily for me, she had experience with boyfriends and breakups, so she was uber patient with me.

He was the first man I shared a bed with, the first man I

had grown-up sex with in my bed, and I had a difficult time processing all those emotions. For me, sharing those firsts created a different level of attachment. With no life experience, I didn't have the emotional tools to handle a very rational, calm, and friendly breakup with someone whom I had only dated for three months. I mean, besides a neighbor "friend" whom I would "hang out" with occasionally, being in a relationship seemed to be for everyone but me. I wanted to find a person to get married to, to build a life with. I believe I am wired to be married and at the age of eighteen, it felt I was never going to find someone ... because of one breakup. My marital clock was ticking, and JR had gotten engaged at Christmas: What was wrong with me? Why did the first person I had a relationship with not propose in three months? When would I find someone to marry? Was I even good enough for someone to marry?

Turns out I would not turn into a spinster at the ripe old age of eighteen. It only took a couple of months to learn this because it was only a couple months after my first break up that I met the person I would marry.

We met at work, and she was unlike anyone I'd known. For starters, she was the first real lesbian I'd met, and I was slightly terrified. Not terrified in a bad way but in a nervous, excited, curious, totally out of my league here, not sure what to do or say kind of way. She had a wonderful sense of humor and a laugh that came from her stomach. She was playful; you knew when she had something up her sleeve because the Cheshire Cat grin gave it away.

We had the typical gay-girl-meets-straight-girl-at-work lesbian love story. It started with us hanging out with a couple people from work and then within a month, I had moved into her apartment. Like I said, standard procedure. For those of you who haven't heard the joke: What does a lesbian bring on a second date? A U-Haul.

In the beginning, there were four of us girls that hung out all the time after work. We would eat Mexican food at least once a week, meet up for shopping or just sit around someone's house and get high.

Once I started spending most nights at the apartment, Tiffy would slumber party with us, platonically, as moral support. Tiffy worked at the apartment community as the front-desk receptionist and has the biggest heart of anyone I have ever met! She was married at the time but always looking to make new friends. Her role in my life has been instrumental. We would spend the next twenty-one years growing together, with her leading the way to true authenticity.

At first, we all shared a bed, but when things started moving in a more romantic direction, Tiffy slept on the couch. Looking back, the groove we adapted to in those first months, the three of us being inseparable with few boundaries, was foreshadowing. I'm going to say it was a glimpse of my future, seeing how amazing doing life with two other people is. Even after we were officially together, the three of us did everything together. We still took vacations, ate Mexican food way too often, and, as time progressed, helped each other through divorces, weddings, and births.

The start of My Wife and I's relationship had lots of roadblocks, including an ex-girlfriend who was a little too fresh, a mild obsession with an ex-lover, and coming out to my family. The hardest trial, and the one that never ended during our marriage, was the announcement to my whole family that I was dating a woman, making me gay. Their lack of acceptance to this fact, and lack of acceptance for her as a person, was the constant elephant in every room.

I knew it would be hard to tell everyone, especially my parents, so I dipped my toes into the pool slowly. I was lucky enough to have a good relationship with two of my aunts who lived in Atlanta, so they were the first ones to know. After several months of dating, I figured I should start that conversation with Mom and Dad. It was already going to be a horrible and uncomfortable conversation, but I definitely made it worse when I chose to be a bitch about it. I first attempted to be sly and show my mom a picture of her and me from a recent beach trip we took with not context. Slight backstory here: My mom and I had not had a great relationship for a couple of years because I was nineteen and knew everything. I'd been rebellious for a couple of years prior (I was not an easy teen) and neither of us liked each other very much. Of course, we loved each other but just hadn't found our groove yet. As I was showing my mom the pictures taken during that weekend, I felt her getting uncomfortable.

"Is she a ..."

"Yes, Mom! A real live lesbian!"

I could see her discomfort, and disapproval, starting to escalate. Just two brief sentences and I went on the defense. Fight or flight mode switched to high gear and I panicked.

"You're not ..."

I just glared at her, almost daring her to finish the sentence, and without answering, stormed out of the house like a brat and drove off. I wanted to throw it in her face, make her feel bad for being so judgy. How dare she not be as open-minded as me. How dare she have a different opinion that I did not like. I was a nineteen-year-old adult, and she should agree with everything I say and do. Ugh.

Picture it, Atlanta, Georgia, 2002 ... being gay was not okay in my family. This is twenty years ago. My wife's family welcomed me with open arms and took me right in, so it was hard to explain why she was not included or why I couldn't just "stand up to them." Her older sister was also gay, so her parents were broken in, open, and loving about it. I honestly don't know how she did it all those years with me. I would have been an emotional mess if I was the one who was excluded from vacations, events, and holidays. It was years after we divorced that my parents apologized, and we had many conversations that have healed that period in our lives. I am even their favorite daughter now.

Before judging their actions, keep in mind a couple of key facts. This was 2002 and while being gay was a thing that society was starting to accept, it was not nearly as mainstream as it is today. You had two cable television shows, one about gay men called *Queer as Folk* that premiered in 2000 and then *The L Word* in 2004 to represent lesbians. That was it. There were a few gay characters on mainstream television, but their storylines generally were not the main focus. It was glanced over as if to say, "look how progressive we are," but no one would take a chance on tanking their ratings if they showed too much. There were a few celebrities like Elton John and George Michael who were out in the nineties, but most others were still "in the closet." Ellen DeGeneres made history when she came out publicly on her sitcom and it was a massive risk. That was in 1997.

To be clear, this period was not, by any means, the beginning of gay rights. A 1962 march held in front of Independence Hall in Philadelphia marked the beginning of the modern gay rights movement according to some. According to history.com, we need to go back another forty years to 1924, when Henry Gerber founded the Society for Human Rights in Chicago, the first documented organization for gay rights. They published a newsletter called "Friendship and Freedom" catering to gay interests. Not surprisingly, there were multiple raids by the Chicago police and it was forced to stop publications in 1925.

It wasn't until the 1950s that publications and groups began to resurface, bringing awareness to homosexuality, but hold that excitement about a new wave of change. In 1952, the American Psychiatric Association decided that homosexuality was actually a medical, mental disorder and officially listed it as such. What is even more unfathomable in today's age is that the president of the United States, Dwight D. Eisenhower, in 1953 banned people of "sexual perversion" from federal jobs. Someone who loved another human that happened to be the same gender was considered a pervert. Can you imagine saying that in today's society? And that law stayed in effect for twenty years.

As I mentioned before, I grew up with the Catholic June and Ward Cleaver. I don't believe that my mom had ever actually met someone who was gay, let alone had frequent interaction with anyone gay. People fear the unknown; humans always have. And that fear can rear its ugly head in many ways without our realizing it's even there. It can cause emotions to overrun our rational thinking. Up until the 1960s, interracial marriage was illegal because of unfounded prejudice and lack of understanding differences.

My favorite example of an argument against gay marriage: Marriage is meant for procreation. By this singular logic, women or men who are sterile should not be allowed to marry either since they cannot procreate. Without getting too deep at this point, any religious organization can dictate what is right and wrong for people to do in their lives, I just won't to be a part of that organization if I disagree. I was told by the priest at our church I was going to hell because I loved a woman. That is when I officially decided to not pursue any further activity in the Catholic church; it was my decision to detach myself. State and religion should be separate and therefore any two consenting humans, regardless of sex, race, or age (goes without saying this means adults of legal age) should be allowed by the government to enter into a legal marriage.

Here are more fun facts to help put the gay timeline into further perspective. The first country in the world to legalize gay marriage was The Netherlands in 2001. The first state in the US was another couple of years behind. The first legal gay marriage was performed in Maryland in May 2004. This was one of the few states to do so, and it was extremely controversial. You did not see gay couples in commercials or walking around the mall holding hands even in the early and mid-2000s. Generally, you only saw public displays of affection in dominantly gay areas, where people felt safe to be themselves.

When we chose to get married in 2006, it was not legal to do so in the state of Georgia (and did not become legal until June 2015, six years after we divorced). We looked at the options of going to Maryland or possibly Canada, where it was legal, but those were our only two options. It was a hard decision for us to make because I wanted to be legally married, but we wanted all our family and friends to celebrate with us, which meant traveling for a destination wedding was out. We began to look locally for somewhere to have our wedding and JR and I looked at several of the historic B&Bs on the Marietta Square.

We had it narrowed down to two venues and the decision was extremely easy. As soon as I corrected the (fair) assumption that I would not be joined by a male groom, the manager at the first place got real twitchy, losing the friendly demeanor she'd had while initially showing us around. So rude. From that point on, she seemed to find discouraging things to mention and made it clear that we were not going to feel welcomed there. I knew many people disagreed with two women getting married and I probably had it in the back of my mind that we might experience some resistance, but I did not expect to be treated like that. I was trying to give this lady thousands of dollars. All she had to do was be nice.

The second place, The Stanly House Inn, was a much different experience. The manager looked a little shaken when I mentioned the important facts, but she quickly recovered. "You'll be our first one." With that, it was settled, everything went off without a hitch from there.

Her entire family came to celebrate us, all of our family and friends and one of my uncles attended with his wife. As the cherry on top, my parents flew my middle sis down so she could attend. This was a big step and meant the world to me. Having my sister and best friend standing next to me made it feel surreal; we weren't just playing dress-up. Even though we could not have a marriage license, we were married and both sides participated.

My wife and I had many good years together that I am grateful for. We laughed a lot, had amazing friends, and she was an integral part of my process in learning to adult. But ultimately, we were doomed because I didn't know anything other than monogamy existed, and she seemed unable to be faithful at that time in her life. Simply put, if you are in a monogamous relationship, I'm going to need you to be just that, monogamous. As in, with just one person. And that person would preferably be me, your wife. There were three different situations that occurred during our seven-year relationship.

The first time it happened was around the time we got engaged. She was sexting with another woman. For those that are slightly unsure of exactly what sexting is, it is sending sexual and/or explicit messages and pictures. This cut on two levels. One, we were not even close to being as physically intimate as I wanted. This wreaked havoc on my psyche, trying to figure out what I was doing wrong or how I could compete. Two, it was with a straight woman who was not interested in having a lesbian affair, but she continued to indulge with responses. What was the point in this game?

Her job required her to travel around five or six nights a week, which left me at home alone while they were in hotels, bars, and restaurants, because they worked together. The things I imagined happening were enough to make me lose all reasoning. I imagined them sharing a hotel room, snuggling in bed, going back to the hotel after dinner, and doing God knows what. Did it matter that Her Boss was straight and had a boyfriend? Nope. Most women are straight, until they aren't, just like me.

I was commuting four hours a day in Atlanta traffic to work my eight-hour day as an assistant manager at an apartment community, which left plenty of time to stew on all these imagined thoughts. I would get home, walk our dog, make something microwavable, and then lay in bed for hours, watching episodes of *Friends*, just to pass the time. I imagined she was having the time of her life while I was stuck in a mundane loop, waiting for her to get home.

I believe your sexuality is determined within your DNA (or nature versus nurture, if you are familiar with that argument). Your love path is already predetermined when you enter this world, even if it takes a decade or two to see all the signs clearly. I also believe that women are more fluid with their sexuality in general, thanks to the double standard society has about it being "hot" for two women to be together. There is no barbwire fence women must scale in order to change their minds about gender preferences. The term bisexual is not my favorite. It has the connotation of being unable to make up your mind, so I prefer the term half-gay. I refer to myself as half-gay because I am equally open to a sex or marriage with either gender. But I am in no way offended when others use the term bisexual. Being offended by a term or word indicates a righteousness in your views, an invisible line of correct versus incorrect, that doesn't exist. Every person has their own truth, and I do not know the background of their stories or lives. Different words have different meaning to different people. I will respect your choices; I expect the same courtesy.

I was not secure or comfortable enough with myself to see this affair for what it actually was: a meaningless and action-less activity that made my fiancée feel powerful. To be fair to myself, figuring out this fact has taken years of emotional maturing. Hindsight is always crystal clear.

As for Her Boss, this was a "forbidden" idea or even possibly a fetish fantasy. To her, there was no possibility of it going further, so she didn't put too much merit into the interactions. Either way, I felt like garbage. Why would my fiancée say things to someone else that she would never and has never said to me? Was I not worthy of hearing those things? Was I just someone who was good at taking care of things at home, and, out of convenience, I was kept around? Was I not an object of her affection that deserved to hear the same sentiments?

This should have been a clue that our bond was not ready for marriage.

You might be wondering how I found out about these texts and why I knew sooo many details. I found out the same way all women find out these things nowadays; I was going through her phone, without her knowledge, for several months.

I knew there was something wrong and she was not being honest with me. Snooping was not the correct way for me to handle things, but hey, it's what I did. In fact, it is exactly what continued to breed more insecurity and fear in my own brain. There is no way to interpret tone or meaning in a text message. There is no way to insert emotion or intention into the words. It was up to me and my girl brain to scrutinize every word until my insides felt shredded enough to go back for more.

A word to the wise, when a woman starts going through your phone and notices there are no text messages from someone whom she KNOWS you've been chatting with or can tell things have been deleted, watch out because the FBI couldn't investigate better that she is about to. I still go through my husband's phone now. I do it while we are sitting together, and I ask questions: Who is this? Why did you say that? What does this mean? Did I miss anything? With him, I don't hide it; I am just a curious person and want to know all the things. It feels uncomfortable sometimes, but it is far better to hear reasonable explanations than to create a horror show in my mind. Violating privacy is just another form of lying. If you must lie or sneak around, something is wrong.

The second instance of infidelity involved an ex-girlfriend, a teenage pregnancy, and the words "I love you." This one was a total shit show. In short, my wife had started communicating with one of her ex-girlfriends whom she swore she was over and had no interest in anymore. I believed her. I wasn't super comfortable with the situation after the texting scandal a year earlier, but we had recently gotten married, and I believed it was innocent enough at first.

Then it wasn't. The entire firebomb started when they started texting and talking on the phone later and later at night in secretive ways. She would leave the room so I couldn't hear the conversation or tell her she would call back later when it was a better time, i.e., when I was not around. I could tell something big was going on and I kept asking what it was. Finally, she broke down one day and told me that the ex-girlfriend's fourteen-year-old daughter had gotten pregnant. Shocking news, right? But I was even more floored by her next statement, which I will never forget. She continued to say that the ex-girlfriend needed her (my wife) help to get through this difficult journey that she and her daughter were about to be on but not to say anything to anyone yet, including me.

Quick recap in case you missed any of that. The Ex-Girlfriend has now asked my wife to help them emotionally through this teenage pregnancy, be a support system for her over the next nine months, potentially help in raising this baby, and asked her to not tell me, her actual wife, any of this. It was a rocky road for several weeks, maybe even months. Once the cat was out of the bag, I was in a prickly position. If I got upset about her helping and being there, I would seem like an asshole and insensitive since there was supposedly no one else to help them. On the other side, I was dying inside. It was a constant internal dialogue of: "Oh man, this is tough, and I need to be supportive. What if this was me?" And "What about me? I'm oozing insecurity about this scenario, and no one seems to care. Do my feelings mean anything?" My wife and I were getting more and more agitated with each other, she was pulling away, and I was an annoying gnat to her—just trying to be near her all the time so we could reconnect. I wanted to be happy again. This was not our drama, this was not our responsibility to handle, not our burden to take on. But she took it on full force. There was never a discussion about how we should handle this as partners; it was her decision alone, and

I was just along for the ride. At one point during an argument, she yelled at me that I was suffocating her, and that I needed to back off. Within the next few days, I found out why her anger was so intense and why she felt so suffocated.

We were getting her a new cell phone when it started. Earlier in the day the two of them had some kind of argument and so she was being particularly sweet to me. While we were standing inside the cell phone store, checking out, the guy handed me her old phone while he showed her how to use the new one. Perfect time to just glance through the text to see why they had gotten into an argument. BAM. All the wind left my chest. I could not breathe as I read and re-read the message that my wife had sent while we were driving to buy her a new phone. It said "I hate when we fight. I'm sorry, please forgive me. I love you." I had to read it so many times because I was not able to actually process the words that she typed.

"I love you." Those are words you say to your wife. All those words strung together are not something you send to your ex-girlfriend that is causing a huge rift in your marriage because your wife is uncomfortable with the amount of time and emotion you spend with her. No, this is a message you send to someone you are in a relationship with. No wonder she felt suffocated. I was always around when she was trying to cultivate a new romance. My bad.

As we walked back to the car, I could not even speak. It felt like I had one hundred semi-trucks driving over my chest. I opened the text back up and just handed her the phone. She looked down at it and looked back at me. There was no way to blame me for this one. It was clearly spelled out. I asked questions, but I do not remember what they were or what her answers were. I cried and cried.

Emotional cheating is far worse to me than physical infidelity. When you go out with friends, get drunk at a bar, and make out with some random person, this is bad. But it is a one-time thing. If it goes beyond that, we cross into emotional territory and that is where the true cracks start to show. Having sex with a random person is bad, but I believe in the old philosophy of everyone makes mistakes. It hurts like hell. It is going to make each person have uncomfortable thoughts and spark awkward conversations. These conversations have to happen. One of the primary differences in a one-time sexcapade and an emotional relationship or "friendship," even if is there is no sex, there isn't much talking in a one-time escapade. Whereas a close friendship or emotional connection involves many hours of talking. In these chats, there is a high probability that someone will open up about grievances with their partner and before you know it, the walls of your marriage start to crack because one person is no longer helping to fix the interior; they are going to someone else's house. Maren Morris put it perfectly in her song *The Bones*: "When the bones are good the rest don't matter. The paint could peel, the glass could shatter. Let it rain. You and I will remain the same. When there ain't a crack in the foundation, I know any storm we are facing will blow right over while we stay put. The house don't fall when the bones are good."

We did end up separating for about two weeks during this time. I stayed in our house, and she stayed with a mutual friend. We would talk daily, cry on the phone, and try to figure out what we wanted to do. It was a great lesson going forward: Do not rush things. We decided we didn't want to get divorced. We moved back in together and tried to pretend like nothing happened. I don't believe either one of us took any time to truly process what we wanted or what everything that had happened meant. We just shoved it waaaay down deep and moved on. That should work, right?

The third time, the final straw, was just a hodgepodge of things that built up over time, but despite her constant denial of this most recent cheating or my affair accusation, the new woman was replacing me in day-to-day activities. I knew, she knew, we all knew. She moved in to "help out" before I even moved out. This was an intentional decision that benefited us both financially, and having her new "bestie" living at the house made the last couple weeks I lived there bearable. She was fun, liked to laugh, and loved to party. She played the part of a buffer, and it was appreciated. The pain and tugging in my chest were still there, but the alcohol and occasional weed made it seem like a wacky dream.

What cut like a knife more was when I went back to the house, one week after moving out, to get my last few items, I noticed that she was sleeping on my side of the bed. Of course, I looked in the guest room and bathroom to see if it was occupied. Nope. Her glasses were on my bedside table. Ouch.

After seven years together and fighting an uphill battle for the last couple of years, I walked away. Neither of us wanted to be together. That was clear and there was no more relationship to try to piece together. This was my biggest breakup, our divorce. I was devastated. I felt that I had strained my family relationships for her, sacrificed so much to make it work, bent over backwards to make her happy, and she could just walk away. She didn't really seem to care that it was over; she already had someone new. I struggled for months with the fact I had failed at marriage; I struggled with self-esteem, and questioned if I was ever a good partner. Sounds super dramatic and self-serving. However, it was what I felt. I do stand by my experience of what happened, I tried to be matter-of-fact in the events and not overly dramatic or try to make her a villain. Unlike with my later relationships, I honestly do not know what I did to cause any of our issues, but I know there were things; I am not always easy. And at the end of the day, this is my version, you will never hear her side.

I could be really dramatic and say I thought I was going to die alone, but that was never the case. I knew, mostly because JR and Tiffy stayed by my side through each depressive episode and reminded me this was not the end of my romantic life. I would eventually find someone new. I was, in fact, only twenty-five, hardly a candidate for lonely-cat-lady status. And I'm not much for cats anyhow. I moved out seven days before Valentine's Day in 2009, so V-day was awful. I maxed out my Macy's card on Michael Kors stuff I didn't need (and couldn't afford), drank more than one bottle of bubbly, and watched two sad love story movies: *Bridget Jones's Diary* and *Notting Hill*. After which, I promptly passed out on my sofa, drunk and swollen eyed. It was ugly. I wish I could say that this was also a one-time thing. But that would be lying.

I have a special black-and-white picture, which I kept displayed for years and years and years, of the five people, all mutual friends of ours, standing in back of the U-Haul truck. They are the ones that helped me move out of the first house I ever owned (and continued to own until the end of 2021) and into my next chapter. I spent countless nights crying on the floor in the hallway of my new apartment, repeating over and over again, "I just want my life back." Seeing that picture helped remind me that I was not alone.

By now, I was the manager at a tax-credit property much closer to home. It was a job that required attention to details and patience with residents. I was not doing great at either because I was an emotional wreck. At one point my parents got concerned about me; so concerned, they flew my baby sister to Atlanta for a long weekend, all the way from Washington state. That trip was one of the best times in my life. She was the ray of sunshine that I needed to start pushing out all the rainy thoughts. So many questions with no answers, so many romanticized ideas shattered, and, most of all, the knowledge that I failed at marriage. I would never be able to live up to the models of the marriages that I idolized. There was only one chance to have one marriage that lasted forever, and now that I was divorced, it was a bygone dream.

But to my sister, I was not some failure or weird, self-imposed shell of a human. I was still her big sis, someone she wanted to hang out with and have adventures with. She helped me see that I could still have fun. That didn't change because I was in a new environment and now a divorcée. It was going to be fine.

I did what any normal twenty-five-year-old woman would do once I picked myself off the sofa and checked my credit card bills. I joined a gym. I would look super-hot and post lots of pictures on My Space and Facebook so my ex-wife could see I was much better off. And totally way cuter than her new girl-friend. Boom. I was fully aware that this was not going to cure my heartache, but there was something exciting in thinking she would miss me, and I would have been like all the women in rom-com movies by that point. Self-assured, confident, and not willing to take back the one who let you go. So at least I had a plan. Maybe not realistic but it was a start.

CHAPTER 2

THE START OF
THE BEGINNING

*"Each of us is born with a box of matches inside us
but we can't strike them all by ourselves."*
— Laura Esquivel —

I had a plan. Not really, there was no real plan. But I had to move on, and if you must move forward, make it fun. Fun always turns into an adventure. Adventures cannot be planned; they must unfold.

I wasn't really sure how to tackle this chapter about my history because occasionally I get bogged down in the tiny details and I forget something big. If we were sitting at a bar and I was telling you my story, I could easily talk for two to three hours, and it would just be the Cliffs Notes. Of course, most relationships can say the same things I do; you've been through it all. What should have broken y'all up didn't, y'all are stronger now than ever because of x, y, and z. That is what fascinates me about love; there is no cookie-cutter recipe to follow. Literally (and I believe I'm actually using it correctly here), no one has the exact same story. I read a lot of biographies and books on personal relationships; I want to know what struggles other people have and how they worked through them. I want to know the battles they overcame because there is strength in knowing weaknesses. I also want to know about the joy they found in different adventures. What new things can I do, can we do as a couple, to grow and create new chapters.?

A very important part of my journey, both up to this point and going forward, is that I have struggled with weight my entire life. Not just as an adult, but for as far back as I can remember. My mom dieted on and off growing up, the typical suburbia housewife stuff, Weight Watchers being the favored one. She was never fat, but her weight fluctuated. In all the years, she never looked very different to me, if that gives you a picture. Of course, looking back on pictures, I can see differences, but my educated guess would be maybe ten to fifteen pounds over all my years. I don't recall anything unhealthy or bingey. She's always been beautiful and classy to me.

My body type (well, my natural body type before I discovered the magic of cosmetic surgery) wants to be fat. It is easy for my body to be fat. Fat comes naturally. I have to work super hard at what I eat, when I eat, how much I eat, and make sure that I work out triple time if I eat cake ... which I love. It feels like I am constantly working against biology to be thin or lean. Now take my middle sister, for example. She has always been tiny, the opposite of me. In high school my parents made her drink meal replacement weight-gain shakes because she has such a lean build. Her struggle was being too skinny (which turns out is just as awful for a teenage girl as being fat, although I find this incomprehensible.)

In high school I did a mild version of switching between not eating and then vomiting what I did eventually eat and was still rocking around 115-120 pounds when I graduated in 2001. By the time I was in my early twenties, I was up to 252 pounds and a size 20. Unlucky for me, my ex-wife has a thing for big women, so she did not mind my hundred-pound weight gain over the first couple years, and I just did not even notice it happening.

Yeah ... I did not notice it happening. I was not very adventurous in the culinary realm, so I lived on chicken fingers, french fries, Mexican food and soda. I did drink Corona Light, so that was a win. I experienced serious stomach issues but did not know enough about nutrition to put two and two together. I went to numerous doctors and visited several different ERs over the course of two years, trying to see what was wrong with me. The response that I got from each: You're fat and need to lose weight. That was it. There was never any guidance on how to eat better, no suggestion of fitness or lifestyle changes I could make. Just that I was fat, and that is why I was vomiting and ending up in emergency rooms with severe stomach issues. I did advocate for myself the one way I knew, I asked for diet pills. They said no.

Eventually I ended up at the ER of a backwoods hospital in the area where my wife and I lived. Country people are not generally known for healthy eating habits and skinny waistlines. I'd been to so many city doctors already, I didn't expect much from this country doctor, other than immediate relief and maybe pain meds. But on that morning, an angel of a doctor took a deeper look at what was happening and realized I had massive gallstones. He did not have an open appointment that day but scheduled me for surgery the day after next. The gallstones were so big and scary that he wouldn't wait more than forty-eight hours to put me into surgery. Someone had actually figured out I wasn't just fat. I was still grossly obese, but I had a real medical issue too.

After my surgery, I dropped a couple pounds because, well, I couldn't keep food in my system for very long. But as my recovery progressed, so did my eating habits, and I was back to pre-surgery weight.

The first realization I truly had was on a totally mundane morning. I went to put on my size 18 skirt, and it would not zip. Something about needing to go up in size to a digit that started with a "2" was suddenly more than I could process. You would think it would have been having surgery to remove an organ that was no longer working properly, but you would be wrong. The second realization came when JR decided in 2004 to get married in Jamaica.

I joined Weight Watchers because the idea of seeing myself in wedding pictures was suddenly appalling. It was seriously the best thing I have ever done. I have the attention span of a baby squirrel, so staying 100 percent on track was difficult. I would waiver between being on and off the program from 2004 until my wedding in 2006 (weighing in right between 200-212 pounds as a bride) and back again through most of 2007. This was my first introduction to anything nutrition related, and it gave me freedom. This turned out to be the best and worst thing for me. The best because I learned water was not just for showering and swimming in; you should drink it too. I learned that diet soda was 0 points versus regular soda, which was 3 points. This was a good lesson because when I later learned that diet soda, while 0 points because of the artificial sweetener, is more harmful to your health due to the effects aspartame and sucralose have on your body chemistry. Once I learned about all that, I was able to quit soda cold turkey, so it was a big win. The downside of long-term freedom for me was McDonald's. I lost pounds week after week consistently because I was counting my points and staying within my allowance. But I was eating at McDonald's almost every single day. There was a drive-through across the street from my job and never time to go farther than that. Subconsciously, I related points to weight loss (which is accurate), but never truly understood the actual point of the program: Eat fruits and veggies, but the *occasional* fast food won't throw your diet.

Toward the end of 2008, I found out what showing up in a gym each week with a trainer friend would do for weight loss and loved it. I had stopped attending Weight Watchers at this point since I felt I had a handle on my eating habits. I have no idea what I weighed, but would guess between 190-200, for a total loss of 52+ pounds in four years.

I got divorced in January of 2009, moved into my own

apartment on February 9, lost my emotional shit on February 14, and joined a gym March 11. It was this chain of events that changed my life course. I laugh because looking back I can actually pinpoint the period in time when the exact change happened. Walking into LA Fitness that day in Woodstock, Georgia, was like walking into a new dimension.

I didn't have a period of time after my divorce when I was a wild child and tried to date as many men or women as I could. I was not going out to bars all the time. I had a relatively high-stress job managing a mid-size apartment community and could not afford to party every night. For the most part, JR and I had Mexican food together at least one time per week, we had another girl's night once a week at my apartment where my three besties attempted to teach me to cook (so I could feed myself) and then maybe one or two nights a week I was going out with different friends, going to low-key bars or movies. Add in working five to six days a week, going to the gym and my time was spent.

I got to have some incredible adventures with a small group of women who loved to party, loved to dress up, and loved to hit the town. This group of incredible souls was the outlet I needed to gain confidence, similar to in *How Stella Got Her Groove Back*. They helped teach me how to talk to a boy, which was a big ask. I'd been married to a woman for seven years, avoiding attractive men like the plague. They made me talk to strangers, in a good way. I was forty pounds overweight still and felt I didn't stand a chance when guys came up to talk to the group, but these ladies made sure that I was always included.

They taught me how to order a drink at a crowded bar. Sounds simple enough, but try pushing your way through gorgeous twenty-somethings when you just want to hide along the wall. One great life lesson is to ask for what you want and be loud about it. There is always someone who will jump ahead in line if you cower back. You must yell loud enough for the bartender to hear you and always make eye contact so they remember your drink. Eye contact in public? Um, no thank you. Not many friends would have considered me a wallflower, but in this new element, I definitely wanted to fade into the background.

They taught me the words to *Wagon Wheel*, and they were the catalyst for my rhinestone jean obsession. I am convinced that between the fifteen or so of us in this group, we not only keep Affliction alive but also Buckle (a clothing store) in business. While they were a season in my life, I'll always remember the kindness they showed me as the new kid and the lessons they'll never know they taught me. To this day, I credit them with the ability to switch angles five times in a three-second photoshoot with a cell phone. My future life, and pictures, were infinitely better after knowing them.

Any good sales establishment knows that you always give something away for free upfront. Then, your client will fall in love with what you are offering and voluntarily buy what you're selling. After filling out all the paperwork for a monthly membership at the LA Fitness in Woodstock, Georgia, the attractive sales guy walked me back to the personal training area and sat me down with the training manager who was really hot, a fact that made me extremely nervous. There was already so much hotness around me that I began sweating before ever touching a machine.

I sat down at his desk and there was no avoiding conversation. I tend to overshare when I'm nervous and while I don't remember every word, our chat probably was along the lines of:

"What brings you in today?"

"I just got divorced."

"Oh, sorry to hear that! What kind of fitness goals do you have?"

"Well, I just spent an entire month's paycheck shopping. I want to be skinny and beautiful. I would also like to make my ex-wife regret leaving me, so I'd like to look very different."

I'm sure there are some additional details of my sob story and blah blah blah. When I stopped blabbing, he pointed over to a man finishing up a session with someone else and said he would be doing my session. OMG. He might have been one of the most beautiful people I had ever seen, a six-foot-two Adonis with broad shoulders, muscular arms, and the biggest ass I had ever seen on a man. He had sandy brown hair that fell just below his ears, hazel eyes, an extremely sharp nose that was slightly crooked from being broken during multiple childhood fights, a strong jawline, and the warmest smile. While he was in excellent shape and muscular, he also had a softness about him that made him more approachable.

After our first session, I quickly learned that Lovie was a wonderful conversationalist and loved to talk. Since this gorgeous man was actually talking to me, I proceeded to do what any sensible woman would do. I started to pay an astronomical amount of money for him to hang out with me several times a week under the guise of working out—duh. I would have spent more than the $150 per week shopping if I was not at the gym, so it was like I was actually saving money. While I made a decent salary with bonuses, this expense was still slightly above what might be in a budget, if I had one.

I was completely smitten with him, knowing it was one-sided but loving the 100 percent attention he gave me while training together. It'd been many months, maybe even years, since my ex-wife really seemed interested in what I had to say, and this undivided attention felt wonderful. I had lost so much of the little self-esteem I had during the last six months of my marriage. Since he gave me attention, I would daydream about him being romantically interested in me. I wanted to be the diamond in the rough heroine like in my romantic comedies, but I never actually dared to think it might be reality. I was paying for attention.

At first, we would talk about the safe subjects, my recent

divorce, family, fitness, my work, etc. Then he started to sprinkle in different conspiracy theories that really kept conversation flowing, along with facts about his current relationships. Most interestingly, the status of things with his wife, whom he was separated from but still on friendly terms. She was living in South Florida, where Lovie was from. They would talk every day and to hear them on the phone together, you would assume it was his best friend. They did not act like they were divorcing. I saw a picture of her ... and wow. Gorgeous.

When we started talking about her, he said right away, "I don't do monogamy." Now at this point, I only know of two types of relationships, committed monogamy or "dating." So, naturally, I assumed he meant that he doesn't want to be married and wants to play the field. He also repeated that he didn't do labels, dating/boyfriend/girlfriend, etc. He would always say he was "hanging out" with whomever the female interest might be at the time. He was against the labels because if he wanted to move on or end the time he was spending with someone, he could just walk away with no messy breakup. They were just hanging out: No label = no mess. I have always been a commitment person; no labels is crazy. But he was really pretty, so I went with it: "Yeah, me neither." It was one of the few lies I've ever told him. And who knew, maybe I could handle a no label, no strings attached kind of thing. Anything was possible, especially since he was not actually interested in dating me. What did I have to lose?

The next pivotal moment came when I casually baited him by saying, "Next month will be a year." It was a total setup. I wasn't sure how to bring up the idea of moving past trainer/client status. Why not try some obvious fishing? We had been training together for a couple of weeks, so trust had been established. When he re-tells the story, he says he was assuming I meant something like a year since I started working out or a year since I started eating better. He was shocked when I replied it was a year since I last had sex. I feel it is necessary to mention that I am still rocking around 180-ish pounds at this point and am so far from the lean, tall, dark, and exotic look that he is attracted to.

A couple days/weeks (my time all runs together) later, Lovie invited me for what I considered our first date. We meet at a local bar, Kayson's, on Friday, May 22, 2009, for all-you-can-eat wings and a couple of drinks. That's right. He invited me to a bar where if I ordered a drink, he got all the wings he could eat for free. Honestly, he was so pretty, I would have eaten the wings if he'd asked me. Lucky for me he didn't since I don't eat meat on a bone. A fact that he knew and figured this joint was a win-win. I don't eat wings, he doesn't drink. Win-Win.

We talked about the same things we did during our training sessions, but it felt more relaxed; I was not paying him to be here. It also helped that I was genuinely interested in what he was talking about. Hours passed before we parted ways and that's when I learned about the world's longest hug. Research has shown that oxytocin (aka the love hormone) is released when we hug for a least twenty seconds and he makes sure to get that full twenty seconds in. Not only does he hold a hug for twenty seconds, but he does so with those big muscular arms wrapped tightly around you; there is no wiggle room, and you are just standing there, wondering when he will release you. Naturally, I assumed that he had suddenly fallen madly in love with me, because why else would he hold me so long? The idea that this hot, albeit somewhat crazy conspiracy guy, was paying me so much attention made me start doodling his last name on my calendar. Just kidding, there was no way I knew how to spell his last name with a thousand vowels.

And maybe not quite that level cling-on, but I did have a whole new level of confidence that was completely foreign to me. I was the fun friend or the cute friend, I never had any genuine attention aimed my direction. I have always been able to make a room laugh and have never been afraid to embarrass myself when I'm around people I love and trust. I would say I was the stereotypical supporting role: funny, pretty enough, slightly fluffy, sometimes dramatic, and a staple in the lives of those I love. Spoiler alert: My first poly relationship put me in this supporting-type role and the struggle was real with that one, but I'll get to that later. I do not know exactly when it happened, but sometime after this first date was the very faint beginning of discovering my self-worth. My journey over the next ten years was a bumpy road, and it did not always go in the correct direction, but I DID keep re-calculating to get to where I am now, being able to share my story—you are welcome.

Back to 2009. Text messaging was still a couple of years away from replacing phone calls, like it does today, but was still a popular way to communicate. I usually had my Blackberry close because I was on call for work twenty-four hours a day, but it was not out of my sight all weekend following our first date. Every time it would ding, I hoped that I would see his name on my phone. Alas, that weekend passed with no communication from him. I questioned how he could possibly connect with me on that level, hug me that intensely, and then go radio silent.

For sure I had plenty of activities to keep myself busy until our next training session since I was learning how to live alone. There were errands to run, phone calls to make, and wine to drink with my girlfriends. Both JR and Tiffy were well versed in every detail of our first date. He may not have called it that and I may not have called it that to him, but everyone else knew I considered it our first date. (Now that we are fourteen years in, he also considers that our first date, where it really all began.) The three of us girls spent goodness knows how long analyzing each sentence, look, smile, and of course, The Hug, making sure we had thoroughly examined each angle with girl brain.

Tiffy and JR were both married at that time, I had not been

single (or straight) for seven years. The dating game was not fresh or second nature to any of us. In all fairness, I had never really dated and still to this day, I have never really understood the dating game. My ex-wife and I went from 0-60 in true lesbian fashion and were practically living together within a month. My first poly relationship just fell into place with the three of us being friends first and already having an established dynamic. There was a six-month period of time around year six or seven when we split with no communication; I went on more dates in that time period than any other time in my life. That staggering number was three—that's right, I went on three different dates. And truth be told, it was awful.

I was given a copy of *Not Your Mother's Rules: The New Secrets for Dating* by Ellen Fein and Sherrie Schneider when I got divorced and it had so many foreign concepts in it. I had no idea that dating was so much work. After my first outing with Lovie, it took a week of reading and debating if I should make the next move (not what the book recommended). I finally decided (with a lot of coaxing from Tiffy) it was totally fine for me to invite him over to my apartment for a movie night (again breaking several of "the rules"). He accepted.

Oh, shit ... now what do I do?

I had a pretty good idea we were going to sleep together. Not because I was slutty but because I did put out there that that's what I wanted when I baited him previously. It had been a year since I had sex with anyone and seven years since I'd been with a man. Let's be real, at the age of twenty-six, I was not super experienced, even though I considered myself to be a highly qualified expert. Looking back, I just laugh, using my old lady voice and saying to myself, "You will realize when you are older." I try not to use this line on the little humans in my life now, but sometimes it just comes out.

I was nervous about how the night would unfold. I thought about how my body looked, would he make the first move, would he think I am a good kisser, would I be "good," what if I wasn't, would he tell people at the gym about it, would he stay the night? So many things to worry about.

Ladies, something I have learned about men (and women too): They love confidence, and a naked woman is a naked woman. If you are in a position to be intimate with another person, there is already chemistry there. They have already seen what you look like in clothes and said, "yes please." You are most likely dressed in something that shows off whatever shape you are rocking, and they approved. They have looked at your face and heard you speak, which means they have been close enough to inspect or see whatever thing you might be insecure about. Hint: Don't point out what that is. Having sex with another person does not have to be about love or deep emotional connection, but it is an exchange of energy. Make sure it is always positive energy. Someone who criticizes how you look or makes negative comments does not deserve your energy. The only people who deserve you are the ones that recognize how lucky they are to spend time with you; read that again if you need to.

I'll never forget what Lovie looked like when he showed up at my door to watch *The Notebook* on Saturday night for our second date. He was in a pair of tan silk dress shorts and a matching tan T-shirt, holding a jug of Carlo Rossi Sangria, and a pair of tan "fancy" flip-flops were on his feet. His hair was tucked behind his ears since it was not long enough yet for the ponytail he was growing back out. I'd never seen him in anything other than black, cotton workout shorts and a black T-shirt with cutoff sleeves or the standard issue blue LA Fitness trainer shirt. I had also never seen a jug of wine before. Box of wine—yes, bottles, of course, but this huge glass jug was something totally new and struck me as really odd. Despite his strange offering and questionable fashion choice, he looked delicious.

We kept it classy and went to Ruby Tuesday for dinner, which was right down the road from my apartment. Truthfully, I really do love that restaurant and am pretty bummed that they are closing many of their restaurants. The menu has a lot of options, but it's the salad bar, specifically the rye croutons that are soft on the inside and hard on the outside, that keep me coming back. Naturally, I wanted to impress him with my eating habits, so I wanted to go somewhere with a salad bar, this seemed perfect. He was my personal trainer whom I complained three times a week to about not being skinny yet. It would be a couple of months before I realized that buffets were his idea of a nice restaurant and to say he is frugal is an understatement. In hindsight, it was the perfect option: buffet style for him and killer croutons for me.

At dinner I was so nervous because of the anticipation of what the night might bring. Or perhaps a more appropriate analysis might be that I was nervous because of the expectations I had put on myself. I was clamming up big time and the easy flow of conversation that had always been there now flowed like dried concrete. I just couldn't relax and create good conversation. My girlfriends said I had a "condition" that kept me from being able to make conversation with super attractive people. Seriously. It was absurd and laughable. I would come into contact with someone whom I found attractive and I would just stand there and giggle, couldn't make conversation. Even in business situations it was like random babble with a few key words sprinkled in topped off with giggles. It was bad. Funny for my girlfriends to watch, but not great for me.

This felt more like the first date than our actual first date. Eventually, I loosened up through dinner. Luckily, he had so much to say about so many things that conversation was easy to pick up and carry on. All I had to do was smile, nod, and not drool into my food. Getting over the first anticipation hump was complete.

Back at my apartment, we watched *The Notebook*. It had been out for a couple of years at this point (2009) and is arguably one of the best love stories to ever hit the big screen. If you have never seen it, a quick synopsis for you: Beautiful, rich, privileged girl meets gorgeous, hard-working boy at a carnival in the 1950s. Her parents refuse to allow her to be with someone "like him" because he cannot provide her the fancy life they need her to have in order to maintain their social status. They fall in love, are torn apart multiple times, find each other again and because true love wins, end up happily ever after. (There is more, but I don't want to ruin it if there is actually someone who has never seen it.)

A couple of realizations happened after I watched that movie. A) Solid dude move on his part to pick a ridiculously romantic movie that he knew would make me happy-cry, feel Lovey-dovey on the inside and most likely ignite a desire to be intimate. Well played, Sir. 2) He had a soft side; he genuinely liked that movie. 3) I wanted a love like that (so did everyone else on the planet) and I wanted it with him. I remember sitting there while his arm was around me, after having only kissed me once or twice, as the movie ended, and I pictured lying next to each other after sixty years together. Yes, this sounds crazy and slightly obsessive, seeing as it was our second date and I had only known him for a couple of months. I cannot explain what it was, but somehow my soul knew he was the one who would fit me. What I did not see coming, or even realize until writing this, was how much our relationship would mirror that movie. Obviously, not exactly, but our path to each other had many of the same bumps, turns, and disappointments as the characters did.

If I was not already attached from our first kisses during *The Notebook*, what happened next really sealed the deal. We never made it through a second movie. Instead, we kissed our way off the sofa, down the hall, and into the bedroom where we stayed for the next twelve hours. He checked in with me the entire night to make sure I was okay and went at my pace. I know I was nervous but imagine being the guy who breaks a seven-year, no-man-streak. No pressure there. It was as close to perfect as it could have been for me. His motto: two for you, one for me. Jackpot.

That next week while standing in the parking lot, following a late-night training session, I casually asked how it was for him. I was trying so hard to play it cool. Of course, I was genuinely curious but more nervous since I had not been with a man in so many years. I wanted to seem like the kind of chick that was experienced and casual enough to just ask a question like that. Yeah, I'm cool enough to just ask how the sex was during a random conversation. I can't recall the exact words, but it was something along the lines of "I definitely would like to hang out again."

Side story: Eleven years later, 2020, we were sitting on our sofa chatting with a new love interest of ours. This was our first real date with anyone in many years *and* during a pandemic. We were enjoying games and drinks at home since everyone in the world was still on lockdown. There were no clubs or restaurants to go to and so the best way to entertain yourself was to be super active on Facebook Dating. This is how we meet Dora.

Sitting on the couch this particular night, she asked about how we met and what our story was. I normally tell these tales, but he just started in, so I let him roll. When he got to the part of our first time playing together, his description of how he felt that night was something I had never heard him say out loud. It brought sweet tears to my eyes. The way he had always explained it to me was extremely casually, "I knew it would be a good time but was not expecting that" or "I was surprised at how much fun I had. I knew we got along fine and you were kinda cute, but far from my type. I did not expect to enjoy myself as much as I did."

When Lovie explained our first time to Dora, his eyes lit up like I'd never seen before. The tone he used was different from anything I'd heard from him. He described the experience the same way I usually do, but he chose phrases that created impactful pictures in his recollection. I could see his eyes actually flash back to those moments many years ago as he said, "I was like ... what the fuck just happened??" and elaborated that he was dumbstruck at how he felt afterwards. He had not expected to actually feel something. Some kind of spark had ignited in him that he did not know what to do with. The connection he felt was completely unexpected and very strong.

How had I never heard this part? Eleven years later, I was validated that I was not imagining things; the spark I felt was real.

So going back to 2009. Over the next couple of weeks, we would "hang out" outside the gym where I was paying him to spend time with me a couple of times a week. It was either eating dinner out or ordering pizza (Papa John's pineapple and mushroom with triple sauce) and then watching one of the fifteen bootleg DVD options he had just acquired and followed by playtime. It was definitely the routine of a "hookup" but I didn't care. I was still freshly divorced, playing it cool with no labels and just "hanging out." The conversation was great, he gave me attention, he always stayed the night, and we had so much fun, genuine laugh-all-night fun.

My group of besties finally got to meet him around my birthday in July. JR had met him once or twice because, well, she is my person and I needed the okay from her that he wasn't an alien. But outside of that, there had not been any gatherings that we attended together. Quick timeline check: We had our first date on May 22 and my birthday was at the end of July. When all my close friends got together to celebrate my birthday and meet him for the first time, it was right around the three-month mark. Those threes have always been special for me.

2009 was a lucky year in many ways. One was that my birthday fell on a Friday, which meant a super long birthday weekend. I have always loved birthdays and believe they should be special, fun, and last as long as possible. This birthday bonanza started the night before when Lovie came over late, which was not unusual. Typically, he was done training his clients around 9:00 or 10:00 p.m. then he would go home, shower and change before heading over to my apartment around 11 p.m. We kicked off the celebration with a movie—or at least we started to attempt a movie. It took several hours to get through *just* one because of the multiple sexual interludes we had, but we finally finished the movie and went to bed around 4:30 a.m. This hour was not a bad thing for me because I was able to sleep in that morning, but he had to train a client at 6:00 a.m. Here was my first birthday gift of the year: He came back to my apartment as soon as he was done and climbed back in bed. It was so magical. This was the first time he had done this. His love language is acts of service and he's always been the guy who does something that he knows will make you happy instead of saying sappy things. This is a double-edged sword though because his actions speak volumes.

One of my all-time favorite things was—and still is—breakfast food. I could eat it every day for any meal. So, naturally, when we woke back up that next morning, which was actually the early afternoon, we went to IHOP for a birthday breakfast, followed by more cuddling and sexcapade's. This was turning out to be the most adult birthday I had ever had. I woke up next to a gorgeous man who wanted to have sex with me over and over again, without me having to beg for it. I was given breakfast food on command. I had plans with my four best friends to go to our annual Rascal Flats concert and there was a pool party planned for the next day. Cloud Nine was floating right inside my apartment.

Several things stand out about this birthday. First, it was the first time I had ever seen Lovie with a ponytail. I later found out it was the first time in over a year he was able to pull it back, so really it was a special day for both of us. His long hair and ponytail have been a huge part of his physical identity for most of his life. Even as a child, he loved and wanted long hair, but his mom would not allow it. Once he grew into adulthood, he was able to grow it to any length he wanted. Several years before we met, he had tried the buzzed look, but he didn't love it. I have only seen this look in pictures but kinda dig it. He only cut it one other time, which was right before we had met because he needed a clean-cut look. This is the look that was almost grown back out when our paths crossed. Since we are talking about hair, I will also mention there was a brief period of time when he had the ponytail so long it required two rubber bands to keep it tamed, one at the top and one in the middle. Ummmmm—no. That was an awful look and by far my least favorite style of all. I have a super weird thing where hair grosses me out completely; it is not normal how disturbed I am by hair once it leaves the head. I am also pretty sure the only males who wear ponytails that long are sixteen-year-old boys on skateboards and hard-core biker dudes. I was not generally a fan of the pony, but he was so hot and somehow pulled it off. I figured, why not just go with the bad boy thing for a little bit? For the record, this was in 2009, so the man bun thing was coming into style but had not hit its peak popularity yet. Man buns are super sexy.

The second thing that stood out was how easily he got along with everyone. Here he was, a total stranger, just chatting away and mixing in comfortably with everyone. It was incredible to watch him move from conversation to conversation with complete confidence and ease. I was nervous because he was being introduced to my closest friends and I was unsure of what they were going to say to him. Put in a more honest way, were they going to out me that I called him "the guy I'm dating" or the occasional "my boyfriend"? I was also nervous that he might launch into some kind of conspiracy theorist speech, and they would think he was a lunatic. I'll never know if anything was ever said, but everyone got along, and Lovie treated me like a princess that night. He made sure to be extra attentive, holding my hand, kissing me, and standing with his arms around me, just like a boyfriend would. I took this as another sign that maybe he secretly called me his girlfriend. All signs were pointing to us becoming a couple. Maybe I was the right person who would make him forget about his No Label Rule. Inside, I knew this was a long shot, but I tried to tread lightly on the fine line of optimism and Lala Land.

The other thing that I remember vividly from this birthday is another slight upward shift in the way I felt about him. I had been excited about something new and all the newness that makes your insides tingle, your heart race, and your words just disappear, especially when you need them. But that day, I took the little leap over the emotional line of infatuation. There was a pain in my chest when we parted that left me feeling like a small piece of my soul was walking out with him.

This birthday was the first time, ever in my life, that I remember having sex on my birthday. And this was also the first time I ever recall having someone fawn over me during a day that was so special to me. Of course, my ex-wife would do nice things for me, but our birthdays were so close together that I always threw her a birthday party with all our friends, and we just said it was for both of us. I do not recall there ever being any type of physical touch from her, outside of a hug or quick kiss on my birthdays and if there was ever any intimacy, I had to beg for it. This time there was a physical connection with another human that made me feel pretty, desired, and I felt every moment of it emotionally. I knew that I was now actually falling in love with him

CHAPTER 3

LEARNING TO SHARE

"If you do not expect the unexpected, you will not find it."
— Heraclitus —

It was a long fifty-six hours between when he left my apartment that Sunday after all the amazingness that was Birthday Bonanza and when I saw him again that next Tuesday night for our training session at the gym. First question you might have is: How do I remember that timeline so specifically after fourteen years? Fair question. I have kept written journals for much of my life and because of this, I was able to go back through and recall (i.e., read) events more precisely. And this next event is definitely worth talking about; it was my first taste of what being non-monogamous was like.

Some might simply call it just "dating." However, the biggest difference in "dating" and non-monogamy can typically be distinguished by the amount of information you share and how detailed you get. When you are "dating," hopefully everyone you are hanging out with knows that you are seeing other people, or at least it is implied. Odds are, there are also some conversations if you are sexually active with one or more of them about protection, birth control, STDs or any other topics that you feel are in a "must-know" category. Beyond that, dating couples generally do not share many details of the other partners' lives or about the sex they are having with them.

45

To be fair, this is also how some non-monogamous couples choose to structure their open relationships: Share minimum information based on a mutual desire of all parties to keep information to themselves out of respect and love for other partners. My experience has been different from both of these. This is how I got my first taste.

I'd been floating for days after Birthday Bonanza 2K10, convinced that we were nearing a new stage in our friendship, relationship, or whatever other non-label term I was pretending to be okay with. There was no question we were going to start spending more time together. This feeling of being desired was one I did not want to let go of, and he was always up for adventures.

It is hard to describe exactly how he made me feel when we were together; believe me, I have tried. The words he chose were sweet, said with meaning, and somehow always what I wanted to hear. The way he looked at me, the way he held me and kissed me gave me a feeling of what it was like to be cherished. There was always a glimpse of "future" in his words, eyes, and actions. He used words like "when we ..." and mentioned things he wanted to do in the future with the implication that I would be there with him. I wanted to make him see me as someone who could make him smile, be the person who helped bring his visions to life, someone who was awake and brilliant, someone who was independent, someone who was not needy but also would be available anytime he called because I prioritized him. I wanted to literally be everything he wanted, needed, and even be the things he didn't know he wanted or needed. This is the wish of almost every woman, I believe: Be everything for the man or woman that they love. We want to be the sole reason our partners wake up in the morning. We want to be the problem solver, the chef who finds the way to their heart through their stomach, the person they watch sports and drink beer with, the ultimate sex kitten that fulfills every desire.

But listen up. This is an impossible task for anyone. There is no possible way that one human can be everything. Not possible. Not even a smidgen of hope. This is why people have friends that they talk to (think about your BFF who drinks wine with you and listens to all the stupid shit, like the argument over why the same lone bowl sat in the sink for three days because you were both trying to prove a point). Think about the buddies we hang out with, sports leagues people join, and yes, sometimes even additional partners we select, because you could never get all the things you need from just one source. The relationships we choose to have for well-rounded fulfillment in life do not always (maybe even rarely) have anything to do with sex. Having the goal of being my partner's everything was not only a sign of my own emotional immaturity, but it also set me up for tremendous letdowns. It would take me almost a decade to figure this out. So, if you are still in the "Sounds like me ... I'm trying to do it all" stage, it's okay. Have patience with yourself. It's not easy but you will get there.

Getting back to the main story. I walked into the gym that Tuesday evening after imagining all sorts of romantic "hellos" and dreaming about possibly even getting a kiss on the lips when I arrived. When I saw Lovie, there was no kiss, but he was super excited to see me. He quickly told me he had a great story to tell. As we were training and the story unfolded, my heart was sinking so fast it was hard to breathe and work out at the same time.

He told me that one of the girls he had been admiring for months from the other gym (she had a very big booty, tiny waist, and long legs) gave him her number and they set a date Saturday night. This date was all he could talk about. It was everything I could do to smile and maintain the calm, cool, and collected persona. I have zero poker face. So, most likely, he was paying zero attention to me because he never missed a beat or seemed to notice. How on earth could this be happening? We were getting to a new place and now all of a sudden

I was being replaced? There was already someone new who had his attention? Ummm ... we were just getting to the good stuff, I thought.

Curiosity killed the cat, satisfaction brought him back. I had never heard this saying before a couple of years ago and it has become one of my life mottos. I must know all the things—always. Instead of guessing or, to quote Brene Brown, "stop telling myself stories that are not true", I realized the truth is never as bad as what my mind comes up with. So, I asked the question I was dying to know the answer to. I asked in a way that was lighthearted and jokey but said with all sincerity.

"So does this mean you are done playing with me?" I could not ask about anything emotional because there was not supposed to be any of that.

"Not at all. Now I can have vanilla time and chocolate time."

Just matter of fact. He can have both.

These words would become staples in my everyday life and ones that I would be happy to hear. But that was several years off. The first time stung. I already knew about his soon-to-be-ex-wife in Florida whom he called "his queen" but in Georgia I felt like I was his number one. Now I saw there was competition for that spot. I was naive to the actual inner working of his brain. I had spent the last several years before my divorce feeling like a backup plan, and it was still too fresh to go through it again. The more excited he got about her, the more I started thinking it was time for me to pull away. Run before I get dumped and hurt. Why stick around if he was going to pick her anyway? She was prettier, more his type, and made him this excited. Here I was the overweight, desperate girl to whom he threw a bone and had sex with since no one else stepped up to the plate. Here's the part of non-monogamy that I didn't know about: It does not have to be either/or. There is an AND.

This was how he started to train and test me. I mean that in a positive way but that's what he was doing. He was training me to broaden my worldviews on relationships. Broaden how I look at love, sex, and emotions. Broadening my mind to look at every situation differently. Simultaneously, he was testing me to see if I would bring drama to his world. Drama is the one thing Lovie will only put up with for so long AND only if the sex is worth it. But eventually, nothing is worth negativity and bitching, so he will walk away. Keep in mind that testing and training are not the same as manipulation. Manipulation is to control or influence (a person or situation) cleverly, unfairly, or unscrupulously according to Mariam-Webster. I have been with someone who was manipulative throughout our entire relationship, and it falls along the line of mental abuse. But we are not to that part of the story yet.

Over the next couple of weeks, I kept flirting through our training sessions and we would still hang out one or two times a week for late-night movies and slumber parties. His time was more limited now, and it was a struggle to keep a smile when he would tell me stories. Stories like how they broke the headboard and how he loved watching her walk around all weekend while she wore nothing but a crop top, boy shorts, and rainbow knee-high socks. You know, normal stuff like that, things you would share with your buddies. I began to think she was what he considered "girlfriend" material while I was being friend zoned but with benefits. We were still having amazing conversations, so much fun, and the sex was incredibly fun. I was very confused.

I was also very insecure. I'd started to believe he would choose me as a girlfriend. I wanted to believe he could fall in love with me. But at the first sign of someone I perceived as better, I went to the negative place in my brain that told me I was just a placeholder. I was the wrong skin tone, not skinny enough, not pretty enough, not sexy enough. I allowed these "poor me" feelings in every time. I can pretend that it was only that I felt rejected from my divorce, but the truth is I never had confidence. It was not my divorce. I told myself I was not good enough to be considered the true apple of someone's eye. No one else told me these things, I believed the lies I told myself.

Once the newness of the rainbow sock chick wore off, things began to shift back to where we were before. He was still making more time for her than me, but he was also starting to open up to me in new ways. He would make comments like, "She is fun, but conversation with you is so much better." This statement from a man who is a major intellectual junkie is a big deal. My confidence started to climb back up when he started making comments, small things that might seem mundane, while we would be lying in bed, just cuddling and holding each other. The intimacy was different from it had been before. I was starting to shift my mindset to believe that he was seeing me as a constant while others might come and go. This was not a concept I was opposed to. I was coming around to the idea of being truly open to sharing, as long as I was on top. You know, number one. Clearly, my confidence level was tied to the amount of attention I received. That's healthy right?

Fun fact that has taken years and one failed attempt at a poly family to figure out … turns out there is no such thing as number one in my long-term version of ethical non-monogamy. Nope. Just not a thing. Why? Because each person has their own unique gifts and talents that they bring to the table. Ultimately, both Lovie and I want a partner who is equal in all things. When there is a stated hierarchy such a Queen/Princess, Wife/Lover, Partner/Toy or even Wife/Girlfriend there will be power struggles along the way where both women (or men in other dynamics) are going to try to "prove" dominance and attempt to shift to a level playing field. My friends, I will tell you from very personal experience: That never goes well. Eventually, you might end up resenting each other and start to see the other person as a threat instead of a partner.

As a side note, I am not referring to courting or dating stages of new relationships because, of course, the dynamics during those times will be different. I am speaking from my own experience in an established relationship where we were well into our journey AND living together. Admittedly, I am not familiar with BDSM or Dom/Sub family dynamics, and so this does not apply to that conversation. This is also not relevant if you are a unicorn who enjoys shorter-term relationships with married couples (We love you for it.). But since this is my book, this is a nugget of knowledge that I wanted to share, hoping it might save even one person from grief and heartache. Bottom line, you have to be 1000 percent upfront with every human involved in the dynamic as to where you are at each stage along the way. It may be a shitty conversation at times but without the hard conversations, you won't be able to move forward.

An even worse consequence is that people will be hurt and relationships can be destroyed. Destroyed. I could not think of a more dramatic word. Think end-of-times movies; that is what your insides will feel like when you spend years in a dynamic that's not what you believed it was. The unraveling of lies in your life is comparable to a building collapsing in an earthquake. Stories crashing down, stones and rubble thrown carelessly through the air while you struggle to get your footing back. It's okay to be unsure of where someone new fits in. It's okay to have questions like "who can play separately", "does someone have complete veto authority?" or "who is responsible for doing the dishes." It's not ok to lie or be manipulative. Regardless of any dynamic, there must always be a 100 percent transparency, respect and honesty.

Anyway, so back to late summer and into early fall 2009 when I wanted to be number one in Lovie's life. The next several months were blissful. We started to have a routine; we would train two nights a week together, he would come over after he showered and then I would call in late to work the next morning so we could cuddle and play. Each weekend we spent one night—if not two—together and went on any adventure we could think of. This time frame was when we were a legitimate dating couple. He came to all functions with my friends, he had a key to my apartment, I no longer woke up to brush my teeth just to sneak back into bed so I could pretend "I woke up like this." It was legit. If you ask him now, I bet he would say he considered us dating as well. If you asked him back then, he would have most likely said we were just hanging out, nothing serious. I'll take it. That is part of the beauty of our story: It has many different versions.

No matter what anyone called it, we were having fun. One of my all-time favorite things we would do is drink and cook. During one of our inaugural Taco and Tequila nights (later coined T&T) in late September, he casually threw a bomb on me while standing on the opposite side of the kitchen bar. I was busy making our margaritas and he blurted out, "I'm thinking about moving back to South Florida." He then watched my face attempt to process the words he just said. He was staring at me intently, maybe trying to see if I would overreact or maybe just curious about any reaction. I did not know how to process those words; I was trying to still grasp what he said. I was frozen in front of the blender, hands braced on the counter to hold myself up. The only words I could get out were "ummm … okay …" We were just about to have so much drunk fun. Why did he ruin it? What was I supposed to say now? Luckily, my reaction didn't appear to ruin his night, so he turned away to walk down the hall to use the restroom. I took the golden opportunity to run outside to smoke, cry alone, so he wouldn't see my tears, and convince myself he wasn't serious.

This dumb idea was mentioned maybe one other time in a conversation that I quickly brushed off. By mid-October he was staying over almost every night so obviously, this meant that he was getting more attached and had changed his mind, right?

Wrong. Just a few days before Halloween, we had gone out with my best friend group for a ghost tour of downtown Marietta Square. It was chilly, slightly spooky, but no one got frostbite or brought home any spirits. Afterwards, we went straight home to relieve the coldness in a boiling shower and got to bed earlier than usual. There was nothing particularly notable about our interactions at home, they were *comfortable*. A feeling that I was getting attached to. The next morning, sitting at the actual dining room table, a fancier setting than normal since I made my semi-gourmet french toast (it was probably awful since I was still learning how to make real meals), Lovie announced that he was moving back to South Florida, and it was happening next week. Period. That was it. Not up for discussion, no more thinking about it, no remorse for just blurting that out. He didn't make any speech, didn't ask or even mention the idea of me going with him. Just announced he was moving back to tropical winters because he could not handle the cold.

I just sat there and blankly stared at him. Time stopped; I had a hard time taking a full breath. For the last two months I had been pushing this conversation away, pretending it was not real. I checked out of my current physical place and flashed back to the night before, the first real cold weather we had, and wondered what about that caused this sudden reaction. It could not have just been the weather, that's ridiculous. Had I said something? Did I remember any moments that he seemed irritated with me? Blank.

The tears just started coming. I couldn't stop them; I couldn't find any words. There were so many words, phrases, questions just swirling through my head at the speed of light and I was not able to grab onto any of them. Speech was eluding me. I became acutely aware that my emotions were as bare as my body, there was nothing to hide behind.

I've always been a crier. Any emotion at all: joy, excitement, anger, fear, or sadness all cause the internal floodgates to release. When I get to a certain level of sadness, the "ugly cry" starts. For those who happen to be unfamiliar with the "ugly cry," it happens when the waterworks are so intensely pouring out of your eyes, it starts spilling out of your nose and mouth at a rate that is unpredictable. Is it snot? Is it drool? Is it just the tears rolling down and finally reaching your mouth before you can wipe them away? Yes. The answer is yes to all the above. On top of all that hotness, your nose scrunches up into your eyes, your mouth turns down like a painted-on clown face, and somehow your cheeks get raised but your chin gets pulled toward the back of your neck. All this face action, my beautiful friends, gives even the skinniest human a double chin. Add in the shoulders heaving as they move up and down, bright red face, puffy eyes, and most likely your entire body is shaking in the rhythm of your sobs. That is the beautiful imagery of the "ugly cry." On the plus side: I have light blue eyes, so once I calm down, I must say, my eyes are quite brilliant when they still have a light tear glaze over them. The color is astounding. You have to find the positive in each situation—that is my positive to the ugly cry.

At that dining room table, I did not have the brilliant glaze. I quickly escalated to the ugly cry; I needed an escape. I was failing at keeping my cool, so I went outside to smoke while the tears flowed until I could stop them enough to maintain myself. No one looks cute doing the pathetic don't-leave-me cry. He was gracious enough to not follow me out.

He had the intention of moving along with our day like he hadn't just buried the dreams I had been creating for the last eight or nine months in an avalanche, literally seven hundred miles wide. Just back to regularly scheduled programming. His responses were dry, short, and, after only a few moments, it was abundantly clear he was done with any line of questioning regarding the matter.

Impending doom was the way to describe that next/last week he lived in Atlanta. I lost interest in hanging out with groups of people. I was melancholy more hours than not. I just moped around, counting down the days until his Honda Odyssey pointed south for good. What I should've been doing was enjoying each second, knowing that soon I wouldn't be able to see him multiple times a week. Gratitude for the short time we did have left was not on my radar. He seemed to be avoiding me, keeping me at arm's length. He canceled any plans we made and would not see me outside of the gym. I was scared I wasn't even going to get to say goodbye to him. I had tried to be understanding. I had not begged him to stay in a dramatic kind of way; I cried on the inside like a winner (or at least cried inside my apartment like a winner). Why was Lovie suddenly so cold and pushing me away?

Turns out his ex-wife asked him not to be with me for the next week so the anticipation of them being together would build up. And he agreed. That is why he pushed me away. They were going to give their relationship another try. Sure, he hates the cold, but I knew now that was not the real reason. The only way avoid sexual interactions with me was to avoid me. The sheer number of ugly cries that happened this week was off the charts. This goodbye was the equivalent to what I felt after I got divorced. That sounds really dramatic since we had only been dating for seven-ish months, but I knew he was my person. I knew deep down that we were perfect for each other, that our lives were meant to be connected.

This feeling was validated when he came over at midnight the day he left. There were few words spoken. He immediately pulled me into his arms and passionately kissed me. When we would pull back from kissing, arms still wrapped around each other, we used only our eyes to communicate. He held me tighter than ever before, letting out slow, deep breaths in my ear to show me the words he couldn't say. We made love on the sofa and then he left my apartment.

CHAPTER 4

700 TO 7

I'd never gone through a breakup with someone I was "dating." Mostly because I never really dated. In high school "dating" meant we would hold hands in the hallways between classes, pecks on the lips, phone calls every night, but nothing outside of the school grounds. There were no actual dates. Fun fact: To date, I have only broken up with one person in my life. All other relationships were ended by the other party. Based on that fact, labeling this a break up seemed like a harsh way to describe what happened with Lovie and me because it wasn't like anything went wrong. He just moved seven hundred miles away.

I went back to hanging out with friends and tried to focus on having fun, living that single life. But I couldn't let go. This was a time in my life when I hadn't learned to be independent. Oh, I totally thought I was independent because I had my own two-bedroom apartment, a car payment for my 2005 Toyota Highlander that I made from my paycheck that I received from my career I had been working on for seven years. (Full disclosure about my car: I totaled my ex-wife's new 2004 Tacoma one night in early 2005 and instead of replacing it, we bought me the SUV. So technically, it was my car, and I was making the payments, but her name remained on it until it was paid off.). If I wanted to go drink on a work night, I could. Being independent at this time meant not having to answer to anyone, not that I could emotionally make it on my own.

I was twenty-six years old, moving on nicely from my divorce, and now skinny-ish. Working out and sleeping with a personal trainer really did wonders for my body. I thought it improved my actual self-confidence, but it really just made me like my body a tiny bit more. There was no authentic confidence. Inside, I focused all my energy on two things: A) Avoiding actually working on my inner self at all costs. 2) Lovie. He took up so much of my brain space that I was not able to separate where I was in life outside of him. I had no real drive to do anything new or exciting. I wasn't fully present in any activity because I was waiting to see if he would text or call. On the occasions that I was not actively checking my phone to see if I missed any communication, I was talking about him. I'm so lucky that I have amazing friends who put up with me.

Okay, so quick timeline: I got divorced in February 2009 at twenty-five years old, met Lovie in March, had our first date in May, he moved back to South Florida on November 1, which was after my birthday, so checking in at twenty-six years old now.

It didn't take long after he moved before he started texting me sweet things like he missed our T&T nights, that he was thinking about me, and how he hadn't forgotten about our plan to try Trapeze for the first time together. Trapeze is a swinger's club in Atlanta that is well known but neither of us had ever experienced it. Within two weeks' time, he had agreed to come back up to Atlanta to stay a week with me. Things were not over between us.

That week he visited me was incredible. He was saying things he had never said before, like "You rock my world. Physically, mentally, all the ways," and "I cannot describe how excited

I've been the last week." I soaked every single moment in. The most incredible part was knowing that for one whole week I got to go to sleep next to him and wake up the same way, lying wrapped up in my bed with him. Every. Single. Day ... for an entire week. I took off a few days from work, and he went to go visit friends on the days I did have to work. Each night we meet different people for dinner so he could introduce me to them for the first time. Huge step.

Life lesson for me here was that I spent all those hours before and after he left crying, being sad and unhappy, worrying over something that I had no idea how it was going to play out. I stopped being present in my life just in case he called. How many joyful moments did I miss or memories did I let go uncaptured because it was easier to look into a dark spot of sadness?

Don't stop living because one aspect of your life is going wrong. Energy flows where attention goes. Find the things you have to be grateful for and just let life happen. One of my favorite quotes is: "Right now you are exactly where you are supposed to be." My true lesson here is remembering those words when everything is not as blissful as I'd like. Years later, I still write these words in my journal to remind myself that I am exactly where I should be.

The week had flown by and now he had to go home to his clients—and his ex-wife. Just like that, he left again. Wishy-washy is an accurate way to describe how his attitude was towards me after our week of playing house. One of us was clearly thinking we were back on and starting on a new adventure. The other one of us was thinking, "That was fun. Next." Each time I would talk to him on the phone, I mentioned that I'd love to come to Fort Lauderdale next time to visit him since I had never been there. His answer was nothing if not consistent: We will see.

We will see? Ummmm ... that is not the response I expected. What does that even mean? I must have phrased the statement more as a question, like I was asking permission to come visit. In a way, I guess I was. I would never have gone just for the sake of going. Taking a vacation alone would have been the worst thing imaginable. I was only looking at this from my own point of view, as one usually does. But what I was missing was that he did still want to see me, just not at the same frequency I was hoping. I took it from zero to sixty every time. There was no in-between. He either wanted to marry me for sure (sixty) or thought I was annoying and repulsive (zero). Let me tell you, there are a million different speed options between zero and sixty.

My experience in relationships was so minimal that I was comparing every move, every situation to my failed marriage. I had nothing else to compare it to. I was trying to handle each breakdown based on emotional memory. By definition, emotional memory is an event, smell, or scene that triggers an emotional response. Emotional memory is similar to muscle memory. When you are in any situation, stressful, happy, sad, intense, etc., your brain wants to rely on similar situations from the past to easily decide what emotions you need. If you allow your brain to go on autopilot, there is no new context to develop a new response.

I wasn't looking at the different scenarios I now faced; I was reverting to events that broke down my marriage. For example, toward the end, if my wife didn't text me back all evening, it was either because she was with people she didn't want me to know about or we were fighting. It hurt and I took her non-response as rejection. If Lovie didn't text me back all night, it could be because he was training a client, spending time with Grandma, maybe on a date with someone new, or simply following the rules of dating: Don't be too available. The correct way to respond to the new scenario with him was patience and neutral energy. Oftentimes though, that emotional memory came in and I would feel rejected by him. Same action, very different responses required. I was on a new adventure with a completely different human who had a startlingly different view on relationships, and I was doing the same things I had done previously.

I convinced myself I was more mature this time around. But I was not actually growing or learning from what I was experiencing. The story I told myself was I could handle a dating situation, and I was able to balance my ups and downs to mirror his. This story is what carried me over the next four or five years. Externally I was fine-ish. I handled myself with grace and dignity (most times) but inside I was hurting and kept the sad times deep, deep down, crying on the inside, like a winner. This was when I first heard the phrase "he who cares less, wins." It is one of the worst sayings ever; I hate it. It gives a green light to be callous, aloof, and knowingly participating in a one-sided relationship that could potentially cause pain. It is a deceitful intention to keep yourself shielded from pain while subconsciously judging the other person for caring too much. It's terrible and while it might have a place in business, it has no place in emotional situations.

January and February kept swimming along with enough phone conversations and text messages to keep me satisfied. I was settling into life without dating anyone new, just holding on to the conversation and hoping to keep it going. I was having a long-distance relationship; I'm not sure what he was having. I considered us back on track, just seven hundred miles apart with no actual plan to move forward.

One Saturday morning in early February, I was lying in bed drinking coffee. Picture a teenage girl from some '80s movie laying on her stomach, chatting with her best friend about her crush while twirling the phone cord around her finger. That's what I looked like, minus the phone cord because we are talking 2010, no phones had a cord unless it was charging. We were merrily chatting about cruising and vacations, just killing the two-hour drive while he was on his way to visit one of the "lady friends" he saw a couple times a month. The conversation was filled with laughter, and I loved knowing that I was the one he was chatting with on the way to her house. It made me feel important. I was the one he could tell all the stories to about what they had planned, be open about where he was, and the small details of his trip. It was a new kind of intimacy. I had a little jealousy, for sure. However, it was not the type of jealousy that makes you angry or vengeful but the kind that makes your heart a little softer because you truly want the best for the other person, but you also want to be there with them to experience it too. This type of jealousy is a synonym for FOMO.

Don't get me wrong. There were plenty of times that I got the bad kind of jealous. The kind where I would think negative thoughts about the other person and why they did not *deserve* to be treated better than me or have more time with him. I would come up with a "reason" as to why I was better than them. This is the poisonous kind of jealousy because it taints your mindset and removes you from a place of love into a place of victimhood. That is a dark place to be. I would even say things that I wanted to be true (I'm skinnier than her or I eat healthier than her) but were, in fact, not true. I just said them to make someone else look bad. Ugly Untruth is something that we have done at least once.

Recently, I was having a conversation with a couple of girlfriends about sexuality, being gay, and different levels of bisexuality. There was alcohol involved. It was late. I was exhausted. This is never a good recipe for serious conversations, but there we were. The label bi-situational came up and we defined it as a woman who is straight but given enough liquid courage would make out with another woman, maybe even possibly have sex with her but would not be considered as bi-sexual since sex with women doesn't rank on the top of her sexual must-haves list. Arguing the point of who should identify as what is like arguing if white is an actual color; there are so many viewpoints and everyone is right. In the context of us trying to define things, my dear friend looked at me and said I was bi-situational, not half gay, because my ex-wife and I did not have sex often. She added that the final proof was that I married a man.

I was devastated, hurt, angry, confused all at the same time. On multiple levels, but mainly because someone I loved was telling me I did not qualify for a group that I identified and associated with. She kept repeating that I was not really that into women because I had married Lovie.

I allowed her words to make me feel like a fraud and felt that I needed to defend myself— vehemently. By the time the conversation was over, she still feeling great on that liquid high. I was shaking uncontrollably, teeth chattering, and my mind was not sober enough to process responses and decided to shut down, so I could not speak.

The next morning, I was still trying to process what I could remember of the conversation without adding things that didn't really happen. I had a lightning strike standing in the bathroom, while going through my beauty drawer looking for eye cream. Holy shit! Yes, there is always truth in what you say drunk. Some things you may not mean, but the overall sentiment comes from truth. She said things because maybe she thinks they are true. Only she knows what thoughts and emotions were behind her words. But I recognized the action because I have done it. Her intentions were not to hurt me; that was an unfortunate consequence. How I identify or any beliefs about my sexuality are on me. Was I so upset because I felt jealous of her free spirit? Was I jealous because Lovie was laughing lightheartedly along with her while I interpreted his reaction as "taking her side"? Yes.

Jealousy takes on a major leading role in my near future but, for now, we were in the happy place, lying on my bed in early 2010 chatting it up about how I had never been on a cruise before.

The sound of his voice and being connected on the phone

together made us both so giddy, we decided to just book that cruise we'd been talking about, three nights in the Bahamas, right then. Like, on the phone during his two-hour drive, we looked up the Royal Caribbean schedule, picked a date from my calendar, and I paid the $600 for an interior room. Holy Wow. Not only were we going on vacation together, but this also meant that I would be flying down to Fort Lauderdale to visit. The next few weeks all I could focus on was shopping for outfits, texting him all the things we were going to do and planning different adventures in Fort Lauderdale before and afterwards. Lucky for me, my job was on autopilot, so no one really noticed. That cruise, my first one ever, is still one of my favorite trips we have ever taken.

Being able to travel comfortably with someone is a good indication of how your relationship will pan out, especially if you are in a tiny cabin with only one bathroom. I recommend anybody in a new relationship, especially with a new poly love interest, take a weekend trip together. Life is hard. Make sure there is no extra drama.

Pandora was a longtime friend of Lovie's in South Florida. Their story starting twelve years before I met him. They met at eighteen when she was one of his first personal training clients. The short version of the story I got was they dated for a couple of months, she met a man whom her parents wanted her to marry and so she did. Yes, it sounds antiquated, an arranged-marriage-but-she-loves-someone-else kind of thing. However, this is really how the story was laid out to me. In the first years Pandora and her husband were married, she cut back on communication with Lovie to play the loving wife, but they still remained secret friends after a cordial split. She wanted to have a baby but, after several years, she grew wearily of her husband and lost interest. As they started growing apart, she began sneaking out to hang out with Lovie again, platonically.

The story goes that in all those years, they never let their worlds collide. They would meet up secretly and she lived vicariously through him. His friends or family did not know about her and no one on her side knew of him.

During every training session Lovie and I had, his phone would ring like clockwork. I thought it was just his soon-to-be-ex-wife calling because he would answer the phone, "Hello Gorgeous!" every single time. It was not until several months later that he let me in on who it was—his good friend Pandora, not a lover. There was never more explanation of who she was or why she called. It wasn't needed. Sure, I felt some sort of underlying jealousy for two reasons. One, when we would train, I felt like we were the only people in the world. Even in a crowded gym with people passively battling for a bench in front of the mirrors, I didn't break my focus on just him and me. It was hard to think that he had an entire life I was not a part of for the other twenty-three hours of each day. It was FOMO to the up-tenth degree. The second reason is that I wanted him to think I was gorgeous. I wanted him to think that I was beautiful and to have the same smile on his face when he saw my name pop up on his phone.

I had never asked many questions about her, and he never offered details. She was a friend who called him, and they talked. That was it. I'd never seen a picture of her, and he never spoke of her outside of the phone calls.

My first introduction to Pandora (aka Gorgeous) was when we got back from our first cruise in 2010. I still had two days and one more night before I had to go back home to Atlanta.

After disembarking from Miami cruise port, we leisurely drove north up A1A to Fort Lauderdale, sightseeing and enjoying the beautiful April day. We decided to rent a room at the La Quinta Inn a little closer to the airport. For some reason, he had an affinity for the La Quinta Inn and this is way before I became a loyal Hilton girl. The price was right, and the location was great. Meaning, it was not his grandmother's house where he was living at the time.

On our journey from the cruise port to the hotel, Pandora called him to get details on the trip and, when she learned we were still together, asked if she could come hang out. Years later I got different versions from both of them on exactly how that conversation went, but the end result was the same. She said he invited her, and he claims she asked if she could come hang out. I was sitting right next to him and heard what he said but the jury is still out on who invited who. Either way, he asked if I minded a new friend joining our party and, of course, I did not. Even if I had minded, I would not have admitted that.

Our initial game plan was simple; make some drinks at the hotel, grab dinner, and then see a movie. We had some time before she was going to arrive, so we suited up and hit the hot tub. Now that I am older, hotel hot tubs gross me out, but re-sort hot tubs are fine. Snobby, I know, but at the resorts where you pay more, I feel they take more care and add chemicals more regularly than the $13-per-hour, front-desk clerk who may or may not ever leave the lobby area.

I don't remember how she made an entrance, but I do vivid-ly remember her standing outside the hot tub in black stretch pants with a multi-colored, sleeveless blouse on. Her gray eyes were piercing, like they could see directly into your soul, set against smooth chocolate skin, and those eyes were framed exquisitely by the long, silky bangs swept to either side of her face. She spoke very softly and called me "Baby" instead of using my name. I was surprised at how tall she was; but then again, I am five foot three, so any woman over five foot six seems tall. She had a unique shape for a woman, extremely triangular. She had broad shoulders, a stalky torso that blend-ed into a thick waistline, and that eventually tapered into thinner legs. What I would find out later is those black pants were hiding spectacularly muscular legs and chiseled calves.

The conversation between the three of us was breezy, and I enjoyed the new dynamic. It was great just me and him, but having another female energy seemed to increase the dynamic threefold (pun intended). The first thing I noticed was the extra amount of attention I got from him. Having another woman there somehow made me more desirable- I was into it. The third person amplified the energy that was already around us because of a different perspective and voice.

We made it to dinner but decided going back to the hotel for a few more drinks and socializing seemed like a far better option than a movie. Who could be quiet in a movie theater with the awesome buzz we had going? I don't want to brag, but I have been told I am an excellent bartender. Primarily, because I don't measure anything. As the drinks got stronger, inhibitions got smaller. The old cliche of one thing leads to another is completely appropriate here. The evening had taken a turn, and nobody hesitated to follow the natural flow that was happening.

Apparently, I was the only one surprised at how things progressed. In those moments, it seemed to be genuinely random. Reflecting back, I am convinced there may have been conversations I was not involved in mapping out how this night could potentially go. Without getting graphic or going into too much detail, I will just account for the emotions that I felt.

I was the center of attention. I felt wanted. I was the star of the show. It felt wonderful. There was no jealousy, and I was amazed at how comfortable I felt with every aspect of the experience. There was a cosmic connection between Lovie and me that was different from any other time we'd been together. I had never experienced any connection like this before. Not even in the seven years with my wife, whom I loved beyond words, was there ever an intimate situation to compare to this. I had never felt this connected to another human in my life; we seemed to be communicating on a telepathic wavelength. It was me and him, with an added bonus, and a universe of passion easily flowing between us.

Every person and every couple have unique ways they connect in intimate situations. For us, it is eye contact. Making and keeping eye contact for me is the most intimate way to show love in sexual moments. It shows you are intentionally present in that moment with the person you are sharing the experience with. It is easy to close your eyes or look around to stay grounded (especially if martinis are involved) but maintaining eye contact shows that you are mindful of each glorious moment. It took me years to realize that he was the first person I was able to keep eye contact with. It is easy to steal a glance at each other or just look over your shoulder to make sure the others are having fun, but to maintain a consistent eye connection while not physically being together is a level that instantly challenges everything you thought you knew about intimacy. Eye contact can be uncomfortable for me in vanilla situations, so this has been an ongoing learning curve.

This moment, when you make that genuine connection, whether it is your first, second or hundredth experience, might also be the moment you panic and realize that this experience is not for you. When you look into your partner's eyes and feel anything—I mean *absolutely anything*—besides bliss, that is your moment to pause the experience. If you feel scared, jealous, angry, sad, or any mixture of this, press pause. At that point, if you have any feelings that are outside of pleasure, you need to speak up. Say it—out loud, verbally. Making eye rolls or hand gestures are not guaranteed to get their attention.

Don't worry about ruining the mood. Fun fact: You are the mood. First and foremost, no means no. Period. That is rule number one in the lifestyle (and in all of life. It blows my mind that this actually still needs to be said, but ... here we are). If you are not having fun, you need to squash it. You may feel guilty about it, you will worry about people not liking you, you will be scared that your partner will be mad at you for stopping the fun. If there is enough alcohol involved, there may be some name-calling like "prude," "lame," or the worst "fun killer." If someone resorts to name calling, you dodged a bullet. Be glad you did not go further. Name-calling is for children, not adults engaged in sexual play. Generally, no one means those things. It is their genitals talking but still not acceptable. You have to be in control of your experience. No, really, it is totally okay for you to pause and reset your mind. And dare I say, encouraged. Not speaking up, not acknowledging personal boundaries will feel far worse in the long term versus those couple of moments of discomfort.

Yes, people will get in their feelings about a potential orgasm interruption, but you have to look out for you and your relationship. If you are new to the lifestyle, it is fair to assume that everything is always a go. But it isn't. For those of us that truly believe in the camaraderie of swinging, believe in the honesty of sharing experiences as more than just sex (or just fucking), we know that partners sometimes need a reset. Something that in the past has felt right maybe doesn't in that very specific moment. Reset. Feel disconnected or "left out"? Reset.

We met a beautiful Mermaid one night. All three of us hit it off, and she was uber fun to hang out with at the bar. The next weekend we met up with her again at Trapeze in Fort Lauderdale where we ended the evening in our hotel room. Lovie was enamored with her, as was I. She was not really into women though, which is always a bummer, but I still wanted to hang out with her.

It was going swimmingly until Lovie gave her all his attention and left me behind. It is natural to give attention where you get attention. I kept trying to reset all night, telling myself that I had no reason to be jealous. I had to actively remind myself that I was the one separating myself when I felt unseen. I coulnd't shake the story they only wanted each other, and I was baggage or a consolation just so she could be with him.

Later that night, while in our hotel room, I attempted a private conversation with him while he was in the shower and she was lying on the king-size bed. Apparently, I am not a great whisperer when I have been drinking vodka. I said to him that I needed him to include me more. I needed to have him make me *feel* like I was an important part of the show. Our beautiful Mermaid heard the entire thing. Awkward as fuck.

Lucky for me, I was not afraid to explain the entire thing to her. Her first response to me, while running her hands along my hips, was, "I don't want to create any drama." That word, drama, hit hard. This was not a dramatic situation. There was not a fight, nor was this a conversation that could even lead to an argument. This was simply communication. I was verbalizing to Lovie that I was feeling left out, that I wanted to be included in all the moments. There was no yelling, no screaming, not a single teardrop. Just words expressing what I needed so that all three of us could have a wonderful time. I reassured her over and over that she did nothing wrong, this was not drama. My emotions were tied to my own insecurities (I did not say that part out loud) and preconceived notions about how this event should have played out. In the end, he understood what I needed and knew I was coming from a place where love and FOMO intersect. From that moment on, after we talked it out, our time spent with her was incredible. Had I not spoken up about how I was feeling, it would have ended very differently.

I know I'm a little off track here since this experience was so many years after our first time with Pandora, but it is relevant to mention there will be experiences that go off without a hitch and there will be those that need a little coaching. Emotions never go away; that is part of the fun. I promise, at some point you will have at least one experience that is similar to this. You will have an immediate need for communicating, don't ignore the opportunity. Being vulnerable for a couple of minutes shows your strength and love for your partner. It is imperative that you feel heard and valued. This is why I made this side note here.

Back on track now. After we had had all the fun there was to have, it was time for Pandora to leave our hotel room and go home. I had an unexplainable feeling that they needed a moment alone, so when she left, Lovie walked her down to the car and I stayed in the room.

I was curious what was being said; after all, they had not been together in many years and there must have been so many thoughts and emotions swirling around, but I did not feel jealous. Slightly left out, yes, but that was my decision, and I needed to respect their time together to digest the experience. It probably helped that I knew he was coming back to bed with me, and I would be waking up next to him. Above all, I knew that she was still married, so there was no risk of missing out on future experiences because this was a one-time thing. Very naive of me. She didn't offer any feedback on feelings she had about this indiscretion, but swore this was the first time.

One thing she did share was that he had opened Pandora's Box, hence how she got her name. That should have been my sign this was not going to be a one-time thing. There was a connection between them prior to that night, a tempered flame that even they didn't realize was there. I certainly would not have guessed there was such a deep passion, but when I think back, I ask myself how I missed it.

There were two main factors that led to my disillusion that this was a one-time event. Factor one: I did not ask enough of the right questions. My general rule with questions is do not ask questions you do not want answers to. Lovie calls this "ostrich-ing," meaning just putting my head into the sand so to avoid hearing/seeing something unpleasant. I never asked him how often they hung out, how close they really were, what kind of conversations they had. I knew she called most nights during our training sessions, but it never occurred to me that it went any deeper. Factor Two: I was under the impression that he and I were more of a couple than we were. He is a man that prides himself on honesty; he will aways tell you what he is going to do (or has already done) with little regards to how you might react. I had already experienced this firsthand. The fact that he never mentioned her, never spoke about her, led me to assume that she was not a very active part of his life.

Over the next few months, Pandora and I began communicating periodically, mostly the getting-to-know-you things and, of course, Lovie. I enjoyed the conversation but was pretty focused on one topic: What juicy details could she share with me about him. What was the insight? Did he talk about me? What did he say? What was he like outside of the personal-trainer role? I wanted to learn all the things.

From an outside perspective, it may sound like I was "using" her to get information. It may also just look like I was interested in being her friend while having the added benefit of learning about him. It depends on how you want to view the intention. Both are correct. Yes, I did want info on who he was, what he liked, what his "other" life was like. I was also interested in learning about her life. I was curious about the things she talked about. She was a new human in my life who had a completely different point of view and had lived a strange life compared to what I knew. I worked in customer service, leasing apartments at the same office day in and day out. She was a nurse who traveled to her patients' homes for wound care and also taught some weekend classes at the community college. She held a strong opinion on the importance of education. I was self-taught with no formal education past a high school diploma. Her relationship with her family was very much co-dependent. My family lived three thousand miles away. We were about as different as you could get.

In the beginning, it was nothing more than an interesting new friendship. Yes, we had slept together, but my attraction to her did not go beyond the excitement of that moment. She was not the type I would have an ongoing sexual attraction to. We had fun, but she lived in South Florida and I was in Atlanta. How far could a platonic friendship go? Conversations several times a week were entertaining, but based on my convenience or boredom when I was home alone. It never entered my mind that within four months' time, she would be the closest and best friend that I had.

Life returned to normal once I was back home. I was back to going out with my awesome friends several times a week, working out by myself at the gym, occasionally taking spin classes, and having Wednesday Girls' Night with my besties. The four of us: JR, Tiffy, Jan, and I congregated in my apartment to drink wine while they taught me how to cook. I have never been what one might call domestic, so each week they rotated new recipes to teach me. No one ever dressed up. We were super casual and enjoyed the two to three hours together.

All time passed without any big revelations or movement during this phase; par for the course was good enough. I missed Lovie in those months after our cruise, but was not moping around anymore. I decided I needed to be an active participant in my life.

Several months later, in August of 2010, I had a random epiphany. I was a single (technically single since we were not officially dating and I may or may not have been more into him than he was into me), young enough to make crazy mistakes, and worked for a company that had a plethora of properties in South Florida. I had always dreamed of living near the beach, and I had fallen in love with the palm trees, warm weather, and sex appeal that Fort Lauderdale offered. There is absolutely no reason why I couldn't pack up and go. Of course, there was the minor fact that I did not have any family or support circle of friends down there but Lovie did live in that area, and I also had a new friend in Pandora. So, technically, I wasn't all alone.

It didn't take me very long to make up my mind; I was absolutely going to move to South Florida. The process was easy and quick. I talked to my boss, accepted a position as an assistant manager in Sunrise, Florida (could that name be any cooler?), and moved into my one-bedroom apartment on the first floor overlooking a tranquil canal all within a sixty-day span of time. In just a few months, my life had done a complete 180 that I couldn't come back from.

I know nothing is permanent, but once I made the decision to leave Georgia, which was highly and *very strongly* advised against by nearly every person in my life, there was no way I could admit defeat. I'm sure most people expected me to come crawling back to the comfort of what I knew in less time than it took me to decide to move down in the first place. Up to this point, I wasn't perceived as strong-willed, determined, or even able to be solely independent. All these feelings came from a place of love, but I don't feel in my heart there was much belief in me.

This move was the first time I had to believe in myself. Oh sure, I know my family supported and loved me, but that is different from believing in me. Believing in someone, really rooting for them, means the words you consistently say about their journey are supportive and helping to guide them (when asked), even if they don't do it your way. Humans are wired to believe our way is the best way but be open to see things from a different perspective. Choose words that are not condescending and be respectful if the other person doesn't agree with you. Everyone has to follow their own path.

On August 20, 2010, Lovie helped me load all my belongings into a U-Haul truck. From Woodstock, Georgia, we drove the seven hundred miles so that I could now be just seven miles away from him. And seven miles from the beach.

CHAPTER 5

THE TRUE BEGINNING

*"She generally gave herself very good advice
(though she very seldom followed it)."*
— Lewis Carroll —

I had been living in South Florida for four or five months when a fantastic opportunity for a BIG promotion came up at work. I was working as an assistant manager at a cute little property when I got a call from our Atlanta office. The Southeast region was going to test pilot a new role for a regional trainer, and I'd been recommended to interview. This position was the first of its kind within the company and would involve me standing in front of people, training classes on new-hire orientation, customer service, sales, the Fair Housing Act, as well as all the things on the technology side. Since there was no precedent, I started thinking about all the glittery ways I could become uber important if I got this job. The cherry on top was if this was successful, all other regions would follow suit; I would be used as a model, and everyone would think I was creative and brilliant. There was huge potential. I'd figure out how to get over my fear of public speaking later.

Living alone, having a few new friends, and taking advantage of the beach that I loved so much were all great experiences, but being solo was starting to wear on me after three months. I was homesick. I missed going out to eat Mexican food with friends and being wrapped up in endless laughing conversation. Lovie had started dating Miami Tina, so I was only seeing him one or two nights a week. Pandora and I were hanging out a couple of times per week, but I was unsure how I felt about her constant intensity; she was trying to give off steamy, sexy energy every single moment she was awake. There was no joking or idle gossip—ever.

I didn't have any real or deep connections with the other people I had befriended and was weary of never knowing if I'd have plans on the weekend or if I was going to be alone. This was all part of that growing season for me—how to be alone. I had plenty of time to focus on eating better (which is not saying that I actually did), working out again (this I did), and I was the smallest size I had been—in my life (most likely because of mild depression). I just didn't have anywhere to go show it off. Correction, I could have shown off my rocking body at the salsa lessons I took for a couple of weeks. However, I gave up those lessons when I got paired with a twelve-year-old boy. I was the only adult without a dance partner. Turned out, that was not the hot spot for meeting singles. I was out.

Looking back, I can appreciate the entire experience wholeheartedly now; this was the first try at my independence. I'd moved there, tried new things, stretched the truth on how much I loved everything, got lonely but was still a relative happy human. When I wanted to throw in the towel for what I knew, my comfort zone in Georgia, I got a call asking if I would be interested in taking the new role. I had actually gotten the job!

Because the region was so large, they decided to make two positions, one based in Orlando and one based in Atlanta, there would be two of us starting at the same time. A new friend! The other candidate was currently based in North Carolina and since she was more tenured, got to pick which city she wanted to home base out of and I would take the other.

This was it. This was my ticket back to Atlanta. I could

officially say that I moved to a new city all by myself, survived, and had to come back to Atlanta only because of work. It was the perfect way to fool myself that I totally could have stayed there but *had* to move back for my career. The Universe giggled for a week or two and then let me know that was not how it was going to play out; I was moving to Orlando.

Ummmm ... not how this plan was supposed to go.

Deep breath—this was not terrible, but I was having to face a truth I did not like. In my heart, I believed that moving to South Florida was 75 percent for me. I truly wanted the experience of living by the beach. I wanted to try something new. I wanted to prove I was adventurous and capable of taking care of myself; especially after how ungracefully I handled my divorce. The other 25 percent was to be closer to Lovie so he could fall madly in love with me.

If you ask anyone close to me those same percentage splits of moving for me/moving for him, the answer most likely would be a 20/80, maybe a 25/75 split at best, in favor of moving just for him. To this day, they would probably answer the same way. I deeply cared what their opinions were. In all seriousness, that lack of credibility was hard to accept. Why did it matter what they thought? Today, I still value others' opinions, just not more than my own. I have also conceded that my move was a 50/50 split. Luckily for me, my plan worked.

I was forced to take a hard look at my motives for moving in the first place when I found out Orlando was my next destination—alone. Up in Orlando, I wouldn't have a safety net. I didn't know a single soul within a three-hour drive. Outside of Lovie and Pandora in Hollywood, I had family in Fort Myers, which was about three hours south, but Atlanta would still be a seven-hour trip. If my goal was actually to be adventurous and independent, then why was there any hesitation about packing up again? I had a good six months of unlimited beach access, tried out some clubs, even tried salsa lessons. It was time to move on to the next adventure with way more money, right?

Right. After I had officially accepted my new role, I spent hours playing out how the conversation with Lovie might go. Maybe he would be devastated. He would realize that he could not live without me and would pack up everything he had to move with me. It was a pipe dream but, hey; I was willing to think positive.

My practice for validating this dream went something like this (imagine standing in front of a large bathroom mirror talking to myself):

"He is dating Miami Tina, but it is not serious. He and Pandora are spending a couple of nights a week together at most and it is not going anywhere because she was still not divorced from her husband (even though they are separated). He and I have been hanging out for over a year and a half. I have tenure and consistency. I have a shot of him saying okay. I just have to ask."

While living in South Florida, Pandora and I were hanging out several times a week. We would go to a local bar or watch Disney movies at my place, go out to dinner, and all the things girlfriends do. On the occasion Lovie would join us, it was usually a game of cat and mouse where we would call him, play coy and, eventually, convince him to come over for playtime. One thing that never went unnoticed was that he would always come over if she asked him. His response was different if I was asking, which usually ended with a 50/50 split of yes or no. She was the motivator. Was it that *she* was the one asking that made him come over or was it the guarantee of a double good time? That question repeated in my mind over and over no matter how much I tried to shove it deep down.

Pandora was going through her separation/divorce at this time and enjoyed any escape from her personal reality. I confided in her when it came to Lovie because they had been friends for fifteen years. In all those years, they never crossed into each other's day-to-day lives, just remained in their own private bubble. Way back in the day they dated, shortly before she got married. After her wedding, she would live vicariously through him and all his sexual adventures. They never met friends, family, or lovers, and were platonic for years until that first time the three of us were all together several months earlier.

After that experience, things changed in their dynamic. They would meet up for their own secret rendezvous now. Both of them said that it was just friends with benefits who enjoyed intellectual conversation and chess. I had my doubts, but they were best friends, so I had to trust what she told me. Come on, I am not an idiot—I would never alienate the one person who had *his* ear and *my* back.

If I showed any signs of jealousy or distrust, I could lose my closest friend within seven hundred miles *and* the man I desperately cared about. This was not a keep-your enemy-close type of thing. I genuinely could not have gotten through those first six months living in South Florida without her friendship and advice on all things, not just him. She would talk me off the ledge about missing Georgia and thoughts of throwing in the towel. Anytime I felt super lonely or sad, she would come over to cheer me up. I confided all my insecurities about how he would act hot and cold toward me.

While the hot/cold trait has subsided a thousandfold over the last fourteen years, that small sliver of his personality is still exhausting. Luckily, over time he and I (okay, just I) figured out how to best handle when he needs "me time". How do I handle it? I ask him. Is everything okay with us or is he just in his "man cave," which is what we call it when he gets into his head. Not only do I get answers instead of worrying for no reason, but this question also brings awareness to him to soften up a little with me. I know if he is in the zone, just do my own thing. I might walk over to him just to give him a quick kiss, then turn and walk off or yell outside that I made him a snack whenever he gets hungry, just to show love, but I respect his need for space. He doesn't need time away from me, he just wants time to himself.

In the beginning, Pandora would coach me on things to say that would bring Lovie and me closer; I learned some of my communication techniques from her. I would cry to her about things that hurt my feelings and I would call her after every spectacular escapade to fill her in. She always wanted every detail, and I loved it. We talked about life, goals, family, and careers. It was not always about him, he just happened to be the one thing we both knew a lot about and could relate to. Naturally, when this promotion came up, I asked her opinion on how to interview well, things to say, questions to ask, and then I told her I wanted him to come with me to Orlando. Her response to that question was a sly smile and "I don't know, Baby Girl."

The three of us had playtime adventures, but we weren't all three friends in the way you might think. Similar to how their worlds had been before me, they managed to keep me separate. Their routine and time together never skipped a beat, but my time with him was separated from my time with her. We didn't all hang out and chat; we didn't go to movies or meet up for drinks. She and I did those things, watched movies at home or met at the hole-in-the-wall bar that was between her house and mine. He and I would do things to-gether on the weekends like the Swap Shop and IHOP or drive down to the beach. But never us three. With this dynamic, I never really knew how close they were or what conversations they might have. I naively thought I was the focal point, the common connection.

Once I had the dream job secured, I needed a place to live. Other than Disney World, I knew nothing about where people who weren't Mickey Mouse lived, so Lovie agreed to accompa-ny me on an exploration trip to Orlando. I had very casually approached the subject of him moving with me in a half jok-ing, half not joking way. He didn't say yes or no, but had laid a small glimmer of hope in his non-response. He might be *thinking* about *considering* the possibility of coming up north with me. It was super non-committal, but it wasn't a no.

We drove the three and a half hours north early one Saturday morning to see my new fancy office. Lake Mary, Florida, is on the eastern outskirts of Orlando just off I-4 and in late 2010, early 2011, this area was booming with new development. My new work schedule was flexible, but I was expected to be in the office a couple of days a week and all of my local trainings would be held in that office. It made sense to start at the building and search outward since I would be commuting again. It'd been a while since I had to do a morning commute, after being spoiled the last six months having to drive less than a quarter mile from my apartment to the front office. From the time I closed my front door to the time I walked into the office door took less than three minutes ... and yet I was still late most mornings. Truthfully, it might have been quicker to walk, but no one wants to perspire in work clothes at 9:00 a.m. in that humidity. Mornings never were my jam, so the closer the better.

The immediate surrounding area was out of my price range since everything was shiny and new. I knew those price points would definitely be a deterrent for Lovie moving with me. He was adamant against apartments, so we mostly looked at houses that had three bedrooms plus acreage. The idea of a self-sufficient lifestyle was my selling point to him. He could start his own nursery and garden. That was the carrot to dangle, land.

Full disclosure: Had he definitively said he wasn't going with me, this search would have been a colossal waste of time. There is no way in this universe I would have moved into a house. ALONE. Especially not a single-story house with my bedroom on the ground level. Hard Pass. Not even a chance. If he didn't come, it was the wonderful life of apartment living for me. I have always loved apartments and would almost prefer them to a single-family house, but he is the opposite.

There were several cute places in nearby neighborhoods of Altamonte Springs and Apopka (this was years before the rental housing boom, so options were plentiful) although nothing that made me want to count down the days until move-in. Until I found The One. It was perfect, and I needed it immediately.

Three bedrooms, oversized walk-in shower with gray and white river rock floor, beautiful red brick fireplace that separated the living room from the dining area, panoramic windows wrapped around the entire sunroom showcasing a view of the lake, a huge fenced-in back yard, massive kitchen pantry, and a fifteen-by-fifteen-foot grapefruit tree with more fruit than any household could eat. It had been recently upgraded with new appliances, beautiful hardwood floors throughout (I prefer carpet, especially in bedrooms, but they were lovely), and other improvements that made this house feel elegant and grown-up. As if it was not already perfect enough, there was a lemon and a lime tree in the front yard with fruit. All signs pointed to this house: It had good amounts of land and fruit producing trees already on it for him and was in a higher-end, well-kept neighborhood for me. Only problem, he didn't love it (which is code for too expensive).

His perfect home was a single-wide trailer or, at best, a small house the same size as a single wide that had way too many trees around it. It was in desperate need of landscaping and repair, located far down a dark, dirt road in the middle of nowhere. Think creepy-house-in-the-woods with banjos playing. If I saw this property today, I might consider it ... because we are married and there's a possibility that I may have been a little dramatic in my initial assessment. But at this point in time, he had not even committed to actually moving; although the conversations started to included words like "on weekends" and "part-time." There is no way I would ever be comfortable leasing a house that reminded me of the backdrop of horror films just for him to be there part-time. I would submit to a lot of things, but scary houses are not one of them.

A couple of weeks later, I had a concrete move date of February 2011. It was time for Lovie to decide as well. The subject was inserted into mundane conversation multiple times since our exploration trip with no headway. Then one night he just casually added, "Yeah I'm going with you," as if it was always a given. Clearly, he had conversations in his head he forgot to share with me.

In his non-chalant way, he said it like I should've already known, no big production or announcement of committing, just acting like he had told me before and somehow, I'd forgotten. Right! Like I would forget that conversation. I was ecstatic. More than that, I was lit up and light was beaming through every pore. There is no way to describe how hopeful I felt. My positive thinking had worked. Now we just had to decide which house to rent: the beautiful lake-view house or the scary-horror house. I was so enamored, floating on cloud nine, that I gave a microscopic consideration to his house. My decision would be the first rational one I made when it came to him in those first years.

Ultimately, I had to veto the house in the woods because I knew there would be plenty of time when I would be there alone and I just didn't feel safe or secure with that option. I had to pick what I wanted; he was in agreement. I put in the application, deposit, and was approved within a couple of days. Just before Valentine's Day, we would be moving into a house together. It was everything I'd been dreaming of. We would be living together, playing house.

As soon as I got the approval call, I let every person in my phone contacts know *we* found a house and *we* were moving in together at the beginning of February. Everyone except Pandora. She had been on the fence and hesitant on thinking he would actually move up there with me. She was never blunt about it but she had a smug way of beating around the bush to imply he would never actually go. I could feel that she didn't want him to leave. I can't blame her. They were in a different phase than they'd been in many years and if he left, that would end. She portrayed them as best friends, so when he made the decision, I felt that as her best friend, he should be the one to tell her. She knew I wanted him to go, and I had told her all about the conversations he had with me about it. She either thought I was lying about what he told me or didn't think he was serious. He was her best friend, and I was not going to break that news to her that he was committed to moving with me, especially if she was going to be negative about it or not believe me. I stand by my decision to this day: She and I were friends. She might have been my closest friend in South Florida, but he was the bestie, and it was his responsibility to tell her. Pandora needed to hear the words come out of Lovie's mouth, not secondhand from me.

The fact that he didn't come straight out and tell her is on him, but she held it against me for many, many years. I had made references to *us* moving in conversations with her because it wasn't a secret. I can only be responsible for the words I say, not what she did or didn't hear. He was going to tell her, I just didn't realize he had not done so yet.

She was furious at me.

Some may think I was wrong for not telling her. I didn't want to get in the middle of a conversation that I shouldn't be involved in, and it was an uncomfortable situation for me. Remember, the three of us weren't friends, we were playmates. 98 percent of their dynamic did not include me. This was not just about him coming with me, it was about him leaving her behind. That was not my circus to deal with. I never asked him how he intended to address this with her because I'm not his mother.

Years later I asked him about his side of this story:

"Did you ever tell Pandora you planned to move with me?"

"Not that I recall."

"Why not?"

"No need to. We were just friends with benefits. Nothing to talk about."

And that was the end of that story.

I quickly learned that with her it doesn't matter what anyone else's viewpoint on an issue: When she gives an opinion, it is true and must be honored with no disagreement. In this case, she believed she was the most important person in his life and that I should go through her to get to him. I bypassed the gatekeeper. This was a defiant action that couldn't go unpunished. My intention was never to leave her in the dark but also to not speak on his behalf, she deserved to get answers from him. This single event, the move to Orlando, would be the catalyst for many arguments against my character in the future. I was constantly being punished.

Even with Pandora mad at me, I can't recall being so excited about any single event in my life up to this point, except maybe my wedding. Moving in with Lovie was the culmination of all my fantasies. I always knew that his motives for going with me were very different from mine. I was in it for love, he was in it for fun. I chose to think we were moving forward into a new realm of boyfriend/girlfriend. He was getting to start his nursery and garden, while still having his freedom, without much financial responsibility or actual emotional commitment.

The move happened in two waves. First, we drove the twenty-six foot U-Haul full of furniture, dishes, two closets of clothes plus shoes, along with other necessities of everyday living. Then, a few weeks later, he brought his Honda Odyssey van loaded with clothing items, ammo, swords, and all the things that belong in a garage.

There is something magical about unpacking after a move, especially the first time living with someone new. Organizing and setting up together creates a bond that makes the space a home. As if I wasn't already riding the wave of new beginnings, while unpacking the scrapbook room, he used the "G" word. He actually called me his girlfriend. This was huge. I had never heard him call anyone his girlfriend. It was another trip to paradise.

I started traveling immediately. Atlanta was home base for onboarding and getting to know my new boss, so making frequent trips there was necessary. I was covering the entire state of Florida, plus helping in North Carolina, South Carolina, Tennessee, Alabama, and Mississippi so travel to all these places would happen in rotation. There was no point in him rushing up since I was on the road Monday-Friday, so those first few weeks he came up on the weekend and stayed in Hollywood through the week. As soon as his shirts were hanging in the closet, I breathed a sigh of relief—it had actually happened.

He is a skilled personal trainer which made transferring to the local LA Fitness a breeze. Within three days, he moved all his belongings in, unpacked, and picked up new clients at the gym. Our living arrangement was that I would be at the house full time (minus traveling) and Lovie was spending all week plus two weekends a month at our new home. Every other weekend he would go visit Pandora or Claudette, the other woman he was "hanging out" with, in South Florida. I felt a certain way about him leaving every other weekend, but it was an arrangement I understood. Baby steps.

Once we were settled into the Apopka house, the process began to create the life he wanted. I, on the other hand, was slower to get onboard, but I had at least purchased the ticket onto the Self-Sufficiency Train. The giant grapefruit tree and lemon and lime tree helped check the first box—fruit trees. It would be impossible to take those with us when we moved though, so we started buying different citrus varieties from The Home Depot or Lowe's and our driveway soon became lined with black five-gallon pots. A tip for newbies looking to start a fruit forest: Spend the money and buy the larger sized pots. It will cost considerably more upfront but the trees will bear fruit much sooner. It took some of our trees over four years to start bearing baby fruits. Bonus tip: Get them in the ground as soon as possible with a healthy mix of native soil and fertilizer.

We got our first set of baby chicks. Jasmine, Jade, Scarlett, Daisy, and Annabelle. Picking out tiny baby chicks is one of my favorite things to do. We didn't have an adequate living space outside setup since it was still cold in early spring, so they got to live inside the house for the first couple weeks, running around the hardwood floors a couple of times a day. We would spend hours a day talking and playing with them. I carried them around in a pocket or apron; they were our babies. Chickens are the absolute best pets. Seriously, they are so easy to take care of and train. If you start holding them regularly as chicks, they will be easy to hold full grown. As they got older, they would run to my car when I pulled in the driveway after work and would come when I called them by name.

We planted an amazing raised-bed garden (to this day, that was still our best one yet) using the square-foot-garden method, we cooked dinner together using what we grew, we explored a new town to find our favorite restaurants and shops, we had a nighttime routine, and, most importantly, we had sex every single day.

The first time I let him see my insecurity flag flying proudly was during the summer of 2011. Previous to this, only my besties had seen these flags, I successfully kept them hidden from him. Standing in the kitchen, I was jumpy because something was off with us. Our vibe felt different than it had been; then it hit me. We hadn't had sex in over twenty-four hours. This was a glitch in my matrix. Something was absolutely wrong; he thought I was too fat. Or maybe he thought I was ugly now. OR even worse, now he was bored with me and couldn't stand to touch me any longer. I could have let these questions fester in my head, but I acted like the adult I was pretending to be and asked.

"Is anything wrong? Are we okay?"

Then I braced for impact. I was terrified of what he was going to say. I told myself no matter what, all I had to do was stand there and not cry. I had asked what was wrong and whatever the answer would be, I was prepared. I could handle this.

"Why do you think something is wrong?"

Oh, god. He's going to make me guess and *really* lay all my insecurities out there.

"Ummm ... because we haven't had sex in over twenty-four hours and things just seem kinda weird," while I quickly averted my gaze from his.

He laughed at me. Laughed out loud like I had told him a joke. He was literally laughing in my face, in a cute, sweet way.

"It's normal to not have sex every day. It just means I'm satisfied, nothing's wrong."

With a shrug I simply replied "Oh ... okay."

Outwardly, I played it off that I understood and was cool to move on. But inside: Wait? What? I was not experienced in live-in relationships, outside of my previous marriage, but Lovie and I's trend had always been at least once every day, if not multiple times. I laughed it off and took it at face value. I think about this conversation when insecurity creeps up. It boils down to this: A pattern interruption doesn't have to mean anything. Making assumptions about actions or words is bad news 100 percent of the time and usually inaccurate. By calmly asking the question and giving the honest reason for asking, I was able to get clarification on my insecurities.

Picking a partner who respects these questions and doesn't degrade you for asking them is key for successful relationships. Had he gotten defensive, I would have assumed the worst. Being defensive never helps constructive conversation because it puts an automatic wall smack in the middle of the "common ground" you want to achieve. An analogy that worked for me was this: Every time you get defensive, imagine one large concrete stone gets placed on a wall. If you were to get defensive only one time per day, in a year's time, there will be 365 large stones standing between you and the person you love. That is going to require quite a bit of work to break those bricks back down. The moral of the story is to not let insecurities and defensiveness ruin communication.

We cruised along happily for the next several months. No big events, just the glorious day-to-day couple-y stuff. Glorious until our house had an attempted break-in, people were arrested in our yard, we had to shut down the nursery, and the police were calling daily to get us to testify. These events put a kink in paradise. The break-in rushed a conversation that renting was definitely temporary; we needed to buy something. Things were moving forward quicker in our relationship with now talking about buying land together.

We started looking for properties with multiple acres to build an off-the-grid life, which included unconventional dwelling options. By unconventional, I mean that were meant to be cheaper than a traditional house. This was a new concept for me, living in something other than a lovely, brick-and-mortar home. We were going to need a roof over us on whatever land we purchased, and his top contender for "low priced" was a shipping-container home. Pinterest makes shipping-container homes look like dream homes, until you look at prices and realize they cost as much as any other home.

Every property I picked had some kind of conventional house, even if it was way below my standards. I figured I could fix it up and make it livable. I just needed to show that I had "the vision." Unfortunately for me, I do not actually have "the vision," thus why I always gravitate toward beautiful homes.

We looked at a fun piece of property that had a houseboat in the middle of a six-acre lake. After further inspection, we realized the entire property was the lake. Houseboats sound fun until you realize there was no dry land to actually put another structure on. Pass.

We looked at raw land in small towns, nowheresville central Florida, that I had never heard of, nor could I find on a map. We looked at old, gross houses outside of Orlando. There was even one property we drove two hours to see because we missed the red flag when the owner said, "Make sure you bring high rain boots." Strange warning when it had not been raining but okay. It made sense the moment we saw the land, it was completely submerged in shin-deep water. At some points, the water came up to my knees, spilling over my just-below-the-knee boots. I was cold and miserable. To top it off, even I knew you couldn't plant a garden or food forest there. Absolutely nothing but alligators and mosquitoes would thrive there. Complete waste of a trip.

All of them would need so much work and money and most were just raw land inhabited by billions of mosquitoes. The prospects were looking bleak.

During all this searching Lovie and I were doing, there were conversations happening in the background that I was not aware of. Pandora was giving her opinion on what he was reporting back on our findings. We would all talk on the phone and I would share different aspects of what I thought, but I was not included in their private conversations. She and I had grown closer, and I now considered her one of my best friends. I would talk with her about what I liked and didn't like, my roller coaster of emotions about not having a traditional life that I'd always thought about. I would share the conversations he and I had, and she listened intently, but she never once opened up about how their relationship was changing.

In fact, I was completely unaware that she was considering living on the property. She made comments to me like, "Of course I will come visit," "Any woman who buys a property with him has to be okay with me coming there," and "I am a city girl." One day, out of nowhere she made a statement that was 100 percent clear to bait me to ask more details. There was no way to interpret it differently. She had changed her mind. But she was a master with words. She knew her words were both specific and yet ambiguous enough that I had to ask the follow-up question: "Are you planning on moving on the property too?"

Her response changed my entire world. She said something like, "I don't think I could be away from him for long periods anymore." And with that one line (I wish I could remember what it was exactly, but I did not write it down), a stomach punch followed by a fast kick in the knee landed swiftly on me.

He had never mentioned, nor had she for that matter, that her moving onto the property full time was a thing. No one even hinted at the possibility of this, and now all of a sudden, the dynamics shifted to "they" were the main buyers and I was a secondary opinion. I had been living a parallel future to them. She was now the primary financial backer, and no one thought to fill me in on the change.

I did not mind another woman being on the property or living with us. But this was supposed to be an "us" thing where we would have an extra. He and I were the main decision makers. Multiple people living with us was not something we had directly discussed, but in the open or poly-type life we were building, this was not completely out of the realm of possibility. It was a goal for the future.

Over the last few months, I had gotten accustomed to Lovie and Claudette spending time together when he went back to South Florida because I knew it was just fun for him. He was not going to make a relationship out of it but was enjoying the adventure while it lasted. She wanted monogamy and for it to be just them, always. That was never going to work for him, so their time together was not a concern for my girlfriend status. Even knowing that, I felt lonely when he left. There was a slight pain in my chest wondering if this might be the time he didn't come home. I knew this nervousness wasn't unique to me or only because we were in an "unconventional" romance. This feeling can be common in the beginning of dating or any open relationship. There is a feeling of uncertainty about how to proceed. Do you call them? Do you ask a lot of questions about what they're doing? Do you *actually* want to know details of what they're doing? Am I acting cool enough to show I am onboard with this arrangement?

As a side note to that last question, I went with the fake-it-till-you-make-it strategy. I wasn't doing anything wrong or shameful, and I never felt emotionally taken advantage of. This was new territory for me. I did not have past experiences to pull from. Each new thought, question, or emotion was something new to the process, to decide if I was onboard, or if I could handle it. It worked for me to put on a going-with-the-flow face, smile, and say, "Okay cool," to whatever the situation was.

I should've been more open in my communication with him about negative feelings and questions that might have cleared up assumptions, but I was too worried about being cool and drama-free. I didn't consider the possibility that he'd be open to me asking the harder questions. So, I bottled up a lot of fear, sadness, and anxiety and then pushed it way, way down. Happy on top, bubbly mess underneath.

I chose this technique specifically when it came to Claudette because she was the exact opposite of me. She cried to him when he left, called all the time, she was overly vocal about her dislike of his seeing other people, and she was generally needy. Clearly, that was not the route to take with him, as he expressed his aggravation over it frequently to me.

I was okay enough with him spending almost every other weekend with Pandora. I knew that they had a special connection and was unaware/nervous/unsure-how-to-feel about the potential for a relationship to develop between them. I tried not to call too often while they were together. We all had group phone conversations no matter which one of us he was with, and it felt like she and I were sharing him in a respectful and mature way.

During this timeframe, I felt open to a real poly arrangement. He would go back and forth between us. When the three of us were together we would play and act like a family. I actually loved watching them together and how the three of us interacted on day-to-day things like cooking and grocery shopping. I especially loved how she would take control sexually.

Even with all the pretend we played, it eventually came

crashing down. He had been down in South Florida with her over the weekend and had extended the trip. I knew this was not a great sign: her recent comments about living on the property, the LLC they had just recently created together as business partners, and the more frequent visits to her house. Apparently, this was the weekend they finalized their plans, and now it was time to finally fill me in.

It was official. They decided they were in love. He was going to move back to South Florida, into her house, and they were going to continue to look for property without me. I was now persona non grata. He came home and just told me how it was going to go, bluntly.

He and I sat in the garage of our rented house, both chain-smoking, while I asked questions that really didn't matter and trying to grasp what I could of this tornado of emotions. I should've put the warning signs together earlier.

My world was crashing, and I had no control, no say. Even worse, I didn't see the underlying signs because I was blinded by my own fantasy. I fooled myself into thinking I was one of the insiders of our future. I'm not sure if my ego or heart hurt worse in the beginning.

Within weeks, she came up for one last visit and to move him out. August 22 was filled with tears and disgrace. Tears because the man I loved was leaving me. Disgrace because I allowed her into my home, allowed her to sleep in the bed Lovie and I had shared, and then allowed her to dictate the last time he and I got to be intimate. Yes, she actually went outside after she gave us permission to have sex, just him and me, one *last* time. In that moment, I felt like it was a gift, an opportunity, and a genuine nice gesture toward me. But after-wards I felt tiny because I allowed her to make me malleable for whatever she wanted. In that moment, I gave her control of my self-respect.

The man I was in love with just moved out of my house and into the house of the woman he loved, who was also my confidant and closest friend for the last year. Double whammy.

There was also the terrifying reality that I was going to be in this house by myself. Dark, empty, and no one to call is not my jam. Every light in my house is always on. I was still traveling 80 percent of the time and often had late-night flights after being gone for several days. My new normal was to call a family member in a different time zone on the way home from the airport, put them on speaker as I opened the garage, and talk to them while I walked the entire house with my 9 mm, safety off, as I opened every door, pantry, and closet.

Silver lining: I congratulated myself on choosing the house I wanted, I'd be the only one enjoying it now.

CHAPTER 6

PLAYING HOUSE

"There are years that ask questions and years that answer"
— Zora Neale Hurston —

The attempted break-in that July in Orlando was terrifying—like the worst fear of my life. I had never experienced anything similar. I bring it up here because the string of events triggered was a large part of how things progressed after Lovie moved back to South Florida at the end of August.

Since I was traveling, Lovie took on more clients in those first months after we moved in, so I often came home to a dark house after trips. During one particular trip to Jacksonville, which was about two hours from us, Lovie called me to ask if I had removed the screen from the guest bathroom window. A) I didn't know there was a screen in the bathroom window and 2) why on earth would I move it, even if I'd known it existed. The guest bathroom window was not a full-size window, but larger than the thin ones that only let in light. I also learned that there was access to that very window from the back porch. Who knew? Burglars ... that's who.

Once we figured out neither one of us moved it, the next conclusion was that someone had attempted to break in. The basis of this assumption was due to the metal being bent around the edging indicating it had been pried off. Now topping the list of my fears was that I spent several nights a month there alone while he was in South Florida. I drove the two hours back that night just so I could see what exactly had happened. Neither of us had definitive answers, so I got up the following morning and drove back to Jacksonville for my second day of teaching. Five hours of commuting, two days in a row, will put strain on your mental clarity.

I walked in the door at the end of that second day, ready to relax. Within minutes, a neighbor knocked on the door. We hadn't met any of the neighbors yet; they all kept to themselves for the most part. Everyone was friendly enough and waved as we rode bikes by or passed in our car, but no one really engaged in conversation. I am a social person, so I was delighted that someone had come by to say hello. Yeah ... no. That is not why he came over.

He came by to inform me that earlier that afternoon, Orange County Sheriff's officers had caught two men trying to break into our home (for what I now understood was the second time) and arrested them in our front yard. Holy shit. My first thought was, "Oh my fuck, I could have walked into this house alone and a burglar could have been inside." The second thoughts were someone had tried to violate our sanctuary, and *did they get in*? Were they arrested after they had been inside, or did they get caught before actually getting in? Had they gotten in before, when the screen was removed, scoped out the place, and now were back to actually execute a plan? I was terrified.

Immediately, I called Lovie while he was training and told him what the neighbor relayed to me. Funny part of this story is that our communication that day was like a game of telephone. I said, "Someone tried to break in and the cops arrested them in our yard." He heard, "Cops are here arresting someone in our yard who tried to break in." He cut his session short, bolted from the gym, and was home in record time.

We learned there had been a string of break-ins throughout the neighborhood and the police believed the men they arrested in our yard were responsible. Since I was the one renting the house where they were arrested, my testimony was necessary in order to make the case. By the time the officer started calling me about court dates, I was back on the road as often as possible since Lovie had moved to South Florida to live with Pandora. Trying to coordinate the court date that worked for me was like trying to herd a chicken into a courtroom. Not only was I constantly gone, going back to the empty house only when necessary, I was not willing to step into a courtroom without Lovie. I had zero experience with the law, had no idea (and still don't) how to handle myself with cops, and had no idea if they got into the house or what they might have seen. I was 1000 percent not going near the courthouse without him.

Since we had broken up, Pandora was not allowing any opportunity for us to spend time together and thus refused to allow him to come up for court. I get it. There had to be so much insecurity on her part about our relationship. They were brand new, and I was the one he had just left. But in the end, we were still on friendly terms, and this was a big deal.

There were several more calls from the sheriff's office in the following weeks, but luckily I was legitimately out of town each time and never available to appear. Eventually, the calls stopped, and I never heard anything else. To this day, I have no idea what happened in that case, nor do I have any intention of looking it up. Water under the bridge for me.

There was never any real question if I would stay in that house alone or not, but the break-in was the ultimate deciding factor. I was absolutely getting an apartment—on a high floor. I chose one in downtown Orlando on the seventeenth floor. No burglar would climb that high. It was amazing, a beautiful high-rise with all the bells and whistles. I had never lived anywhere so fancy. There was a side view of Lake Eola, floor-to-ceiling windows in the bedroom and living room that let in massive amounts of light, a huge walk-in closet, and a bathroom that made me feel elegant. There was a rooftop pool (which I never swam in) and there were cafes, bars, stores, and a library within walking distance. This was my chance to really live it up; my *Sex in the City* opportunity. My confidence had taken a hit since he left, but I was an uber successful corporate woman who could now live "the high life." I had a gorgeous apartment that was very expensive and traveled weekly through different airports to very important meetings and train people how to be successful.

Turns out, I am not a city girl. I tried to branch out a couple times but usually ended up reading a book while dining alone, drinking alone, awkwardly at the bar, without meeting anyone or trying to act like I belonged while feeling like a total loser. Orlando is a very transient city where people from all over the world vacation at Disney World or Universal, business people come for large conferences and, of course, all the college kids at UCF are living the dream there. I was twenty-eight (about six years above the college age to be cool), traveled 85 percent of the time (there was no time to be a "regular" anywhere), and pitifully pining for my ex-boyfriend.

South Florida was one of the areas that I traveled to on a regular basis. Pandora and I were communing periodically via phone or text and would meet up for dinner when I was down there. We tried to keep the conversation light and focused on work, school, and other "safe" subjects.

I constantly questioned my motives. Did I actually want to see and spend time with her? Was I lonely and just saw her because it was better than being alone? Was I using her as a way to get a connection to him? Unsure. I was still hurt and angry because she had "stolen" him away. But a part of me also wanted her friendship.

My entire life I have felt conflicted when I have to make a definitive decision. It could be as simple as deciding to wear jeans or yoga pants or as complex as should I quit my job or not. I see things in fifty shades of gray. Rarely is it black and white. When it came to seeing Pandora, I don't think it was any one of those questions more than another. All three would equally swirl around me at any given moment. I missed her and our conversation when she was unavailable or it had been a while since our last talk. Traveling created ample opportunity for solitude and any human to drink with is better than no human to drink with. And, yes, she was the only source I had to get news about what was happening in his life.

After the first couple of trips down, she started to include him in our meet ups. It was awkward for me once Lovie started to come along with her. What the hell was I doing here? Why am I sitting at an IHOP with my ex-boyfriend and his new girlfriend, who is also my close friend? Is there anything good that can come out of this?

It quickly progressed to the three of us having drinks and ending up in some form of fabulous sexual escapade. I mean, it escalated really quick. Within a couple weeks, I started booking hotels close to their house instead of near work because inevitably the night would end up in a slumber party. By the winter of 2011, the hotel stays got less frequent, I always ended up at the house. This routine continued for four or five months

One nondescript trip in March 2012, I walked into the house and there was a cleared-out section of closet. Pandora gave me a huge smile and said it was so I wouldn't have to travel back and forth with so much stuff. Whoa! Just "wow" was all I could think. We had not had any direct conversations about having space to put my clothes, I was perfectly content living out of my suitcase. I had not asked or even insinuated we were at a point to discuss even having a toothbrush in the bathroom. This act was her way of slowly bringing me into the inner family circle.

The Hollywood house, as it was referred to then (and still is called on the occasion that a memory requires), was a three-bedroom ranch with a walled-in Florida room. This style of home is very common in South Florida. Generally, a Florida room is an additional space that is sunken down into the floor, requiring an ever so slight step down, has three walls containing copious amounts of windows, and is open on the fourth side to the traditional living room, like a sunroom but somehow different. There were two bedrooms at the end of a narrow hall, one was the master bedroom (this was the primary room for our initial playdates when I would leave before morning time). The second room at the back was used as a library/office. At the front of that hallway, where the front door, kitchen and living room all intersected, was the third bedroom. It was used as the slumber party room because it accommodated two queen mattresses, pushed together in order to create one giant bed. None of us were small people; a king bed worked, but why not use the extra space if it was available? This became our bedroom since I was staying the night more frequently. This was also the room where my closet was. As a bonus, since the mattresses were just on the floor, they could easily be moved into the Florida room for movie nights and thus became known as Bed Island. Bed Island was magical and could float to any room of the house we deemed fit.

I say "we" but really I was just along for the ride. I was there for their enjoyment. Every activity, every action, literally *everything* was contingent on her being happy. Reading this might make some of you question why I'd want to stay around, why I would want to be a "pawn," as some of my friends called it. The answer is both simple and complex. The simple answer is that they were a couple. I was the ex who was, essentially, the third wheel and therefore not part of the inner crowd. If I wanted to hang around, I had to just follow the leader.

This is no different from a single person making exceptions and being less verbal during the early phases of dating someone new. When you meet a person with whom you have chemistry, you are 100 percent more willing to go with the flow. Do you stomp and pout at any mention of eating Mexican food because you hate it if your new love interest adores cheese dip and margs? Of course not. You suck it up the first time or two, then maybe mention Mexican isn't your favorite the third or fourth time and get really honest, around the fifth time they ask you, that you despise Mexican food. No one, at least not the majority, comes out of the gate complaining or demanding to do something different. And we definitely do not verbalize if we are not getting enough attention or being include enough in those early months. The other person would probably run away. There is a period of time when you leave space to learn new things. You sit back and take it all in, there's a chess match being played and you have to find your stratagy. If you are that person who comes out of the gate strong and forceful, bless you. You are a rare breed—and possibly still single.

The more complex answers to why I accepted this situation are what make polyamory and monogamy differ. I knew I wanted into the family. I also knew they had discussed having a girlfriend, so it was in the scope of possibilities they would choose me. When a couple is looking to bring in more people to their relationship, it has to jive in a way that fits their unique dynamic. This might be considered courting. You aren't dating yet but there has been flirty conversation that teeters on futuristic without having any tone of commitment. I am not talking about a unicorn to play with for a short period of time. For those that don't know that reference, a unicorn is a single female open to no-strings-attached sexual escapades with a couple. In our case, I am talking about essentially adding four more dynamics to Lovie and Pandora's current relationship.

Four? Yup ... four. In our particular situation, it would mean 1) adding in my role to their duo, 2) a new romantic partnership between Pandora and me, 3) a new dynamic between Lovie and me and 4) it would change the dynamic between them. There were adjustments that I had to make. Back in earlier times when Pandora and I would invite Lovie to my apartment for surprise escapades, I was seen as the primary reason for the get-together. Now, I was the auxiliary piece in their newly established life.

Every partnership has its own set of rules or guidelines. Each guideline should be clearly communicated and agreed upon by each individual participating. The first of many major guidelines that threw me for a loop was the expectation of moving our sleeping positions when she got up in the mornings.

During our un-official courtship phase, which was when my clothes had a place to hang, Pandora was actively working on her fitness and weight goals. Each morning she would wake up at dawn-thirty and go for a walk. This meant that Lovie and I were still sleeping, a situation that she was not having. Each morning she would get up to go walk, I would relocate from bed island to the couch and continue sleeping. At first, I had no qualms about it. It just made sense because I wanted to make sure that she was comfortable and didn't worry about Lovie and me playing or snuggling. I agreed that it made sense for our current situation. Was it my preference? Of course not. I made a short-term accommodation towards the long-term goal—a family dynamic that was equal and based on love, trust, and open communication.

In May 2012, I broke my lease in Orlando, moved all my stuff into Pods, and officially become a live-in girlfriend. However, as our dynamic changed into a more fluid and defined one, the sleeping arrangements did not. We all slept on bed island, but every morning she went walking and I moved to the couch. Over time, I began to question why she still needed me to do this. I was all but ignoring Lovie physically, making sure that I sided with her in every discussion, doted on her constantly, and put in a conscious effort to show my commitment *to her*.

Hindsight is always 20/20. Today, I understand why she may have felt this way. I would be overflowing with FOMO at the prospect of leaving Lovie in bed with another woman. Would I be jealous that there was an alternative connection happening or would I just be scared of missing out on fun? Most likely both. Even though I can understand some of her reasoning now, I can't understand her mindset. I would never ask the other woman, whom I invited into our bed, to move to the couch, just because I was getting up.

I began to resent having to do this. It showed a lack of trust towards both of us. Then again, maybe her mistrust was justified. Pandora was so adamant against us having any type of physical or emotional connection, Lovie and I resorted to hiding all affection. We waited until she wasn't around to steal a kiss or embrace each other. We were like teenagers determined to find a way to do things we were forbidden to do. It's a vicious circle: If she trusted us, we could have been physical in front of her, at her pace. Since she didn't trust us, we did it behind her back, leading to an actual reason for the distrust. Not a good start.

This was my first point of contention. It also led to the realization of our actual triangle dynamic. She verbalized this thought in a random conversation one afternoon, sitting in the driveway after we had been out running errands in Miami. I was caught completely off guard.

I've never been strong at "in-the-moment" verbalizations of emotions or thoughts. I tend to give an initial response that will pacify the immediate moment, even if it's not what I truly feel. I am a processor. I need time to gather my emotion, to put my words into coherent sentences, and have responses ready for rebuttals so I can elaborate on my point of view. I need to think things through. Pandora, she spoke her mind immediately. And right in that moment, she did so in a terrifying way. I didn't feel like an equal participant in the conversation. Not only was I blindsided, I had no indication the conversation was going to turn this direction, but our communication styles were different. It was always a verbal competition to her. I need time to think because I know you can never take back words. Her tactic: Crush and make the other person surrender by gaslighting.

This is not all on her. I didn't see myself as worthy of being her equal in any way, conversational or in life. I wanted to be equals but had the mindset Pandora was better than me. She had multiple college degrees, whereas I had a great job that paid decent but no college degree to show. She was outspoken, I was timid and didn't want to rock the boat (avoid confrontation at all costs). She was beautiful, plus sized, and owned it. I was hyperaware of every flaw, scar, and stretch mark on my average-size frame that was gently padded with a layer of fluff. She was somewhat combative, while I was considered submissive. Her words oozed with a confusing mix of condescension and sympathy that would make even the most confident person question what they were hearing.

This particular afternoon, when the topic of our dynamic exploded, she matter-of-factly stated our triangle of desire. He wanted her. She wanted me. I wanted him. Half of me thought she mentioned it to show that she really cared about me. When she said that she wanted me, I felt special, like there was some deeper connection she and I had that transcended anything either of us could have with just Lovie. The other half felt like it was a jab. She was letting me know that he was not interested in a relationship with me; he only wanted her, and I was the byproduct of her desire.

Ultimately, I determined it was a jab. It was a deliberate attempt to make sure I knew that he was only there for her and if I wanted to stay in the picture, I too needed to only be there for her. She had also lobbed a fastball at me that was intended to hit where I was most vulnerable, Lovie. This time period in our life together was about establishing dominance: Who was the alpha? Clearly it was not me so there was nothing to prove. The odd thing about this was that I did not want to be alpha. I did not want to be top dog or loved more than her. I just wanted to be loved. Period. I wanted to be pampered and doted on. I wanted to earn respect as a partner. I said what she wanted to hear that day so that the conversation could end quickly. As time progressed, I began to believe that I was only valuable as a second, not worthy as an equal. She was sweet and amazing to me 80 percent of the time and, at the beginning, that was enough. I knew I wanted a fast track to family. My emotions for her were real. I needed to work harder to make her believe that.

The conversations I had with Lovie about the dynamic were quite different. We talked about his feelings for me and mine for him. Of course, I tamed mine so as not to seem too eager. We agreed she needed to be more comfortable before we verbalized to her that we saw all of us connected, not individually linked to her. There was a romantic idea that once she knew we cared for her, that as our love for her grew, she would adjust to the dynamic we craved. We figured that if we made every attempt in this season of our relationship to make it all about her, make sure she was 1000 percent comfortable about everyone's motives, that eventually she would loosen up her rules and come to view each relationship as equal.

I keep using the word equal. The definition of equal according to Webster's Dictionary has four meanings but two of those apply to my story: 1) regarding or affecting all objects in the same way 2) impartial and free from extremes.

Relating to the three of us, "same" meant acknowledging we were all in this together and shared a common love for each other in a capacity that wasn't different between one partner or the other. The "free from extremes" was the hard part. Was it extreme for her to request I move to the sofa? At this early phase, I believed no. But as time went on, the rules did not disappear. As our relationship developed, the same rules started to seem less reasonable.

The biggest extremes came in the different ways Pandora communicated with Lovie and me, respectively. To be more specific, the words she used in expressing the direction she saw our dynamic headed. In our two years together as a triad, Lovie and I received very different information from her on her wants, needs, and how she saw our family. This became strikingly evident one night in August when they celebrated their one-year anniversary.

I am big on anniversaries. They are important milestones that should be celebrated. Each year should have a celebratory acknowledgment that you worked hard and continue to choose to do life together. It is a re-commitment that you are still in, for better or worse, through thick and thin. You don't have to be married to commit to those ideals. No one wants to be in a long-term relationship without knowing it will end in commitment, even if legal marriage is not your jam. Marriage is not for everyone. There are many couples I have known in my life who said "why fix what's not broken" or "I don't need the government to tell me my relationship is valid." I applaud these relationships. I happen to be in a team marriage but support any type of commitment that individuals make to each other.

On their one-year anniversary in August 2012, they went to downtown Hollywood Beach, and I stayed home. This was an important part of nurturing their individual relationship. Of course, my FOMO kicked in—duh. But I respected their time together. I spent the evening on the sofa, snacking on everything I could find, and a tightness in my chest from the anxiety of wondering what was happening without me. Watching TV helped distract me, especially since I could watch anything I wanted—trash TV for the win—while reminding myself that it was important for them to have alone time.

The moment that door opened, I jumped up and ran over to hug them both. I had just spent the entire night checking the clock, counting the minutes until I could hear every single detail. I asked all kinds of questions: What did they do, where did they go, how was the food, did they enjoy it? It was brick-oven pizza on the Hollywood Boardwalk, which got mixed reviews and was followed by a hand-holding walk on the beach. Kinda vague, but okay. Then the hammer dropped.

And I mean sledgehammer.

She announced that he had proposed.

I thought I wanted this for them, but my heart inexplicably sank. I stood in the doorway between the Florida room and living room, frozen from shock. There had been various random conversations alluding to marriage, but nothing more than future goals. I knew it was inevitable. It was expected down the road and I was excited about the prospect. But it had only been one year. For the record, I don't necessarily believe there is a standard timeline for dating, engagements, marriages, or babies. Some know after three dates and others after three years. I don't know the intricacies of other people's relationships, so who am I to judge what works for them? This was different though. I knew all the things ... one year was too soon.

The hardest thing for me to grasp was that I was under the illusion that I'd be involved in this process. I wasn't given any indication that I would or should be included, but, as a member of this family, I was entitled to be involved. AND more importantly, I am awesome at planning special events, parties, holidays or anything themed. Making people smile is my happy space. Thinking about their engagement, I figured he would tell me first. He would get my input on a ring and how to create the most magical experience ever. It never occurred to me that I would be the last to know. Certainly, I never expected to take the news as a kick in the stomach.

Pandora explained that while there was no ring yet, Lovie had gotten down on one knee on the beach and said, "Will you marry me?" Her description was somewhat vague, but it must have been awkward to tell her girlfriend she just got engaged to the boyfriend. He stood by, smiling, but did not comment on any of the evening's events. I didn't know what to say. On one hand, I was happy for them. Being engaged meant they were in it for the long haul, one relationship I didn't have to worry about. On the other hand, where did that leave me? Up until this point, we had chosen not to label anything. I didn't verbalize my desires or speak freely about how I envisioned our future. I tried to shove those specifics so far down that I had started to actually think maybe I wasn't a labels person. But like every emotion that you try to shove way, way down, eventually it comes to the surface in a spectacular fashion.

CHAPTER 7

FAMILY TIES

When their engagement happened in August, we'd already been searching for a property to start our family homestead.

The previous year, 2011, while Lovie and I were still together in Orlando, they were looking for a parcel of raw land in south central Florida. I knew about it, although I was not involved in any of the purchasing conversations. Pandora was apparently going to be the financial backer for us. She sold it to me as a "business arrangement" because she did not want to ever be told by one of his girlfriends that she could not visit. Her solution was that if she owned it with him, she had full rights to the property. Fast forward, I can see now I missed that big red flag.

By the time I moved into the Hollywood House in 2012, they had purchased two and a half acres of raw land along with a shipping container to build a tiny home. I felt betrayed when they told me about this land purchase. How had I not known about it and how had they kept it a "secret"? Technically, Lovie and I were still together when this purchase started; I just hadn't been informed of their relationship yet. I pushed the feelings of betrayal deep, deep down. It's fine. They didn't actually purchase it until after he left Orlando, so once I was included in the conversation, I chose to just forget it. I let it go. At this point, the three of us were a team.

Now was the fun part: finding ideas for shipping container homes that worked for our Family. This type of creative process has thrilled me ever since I was young. Growing up, my sisters and I would cut up magazines to make our dream homes. I'd spend days picking out the right crystal chandelier to hang over a claw-foot tub and debate for hours on which twelve-seat dining room table had the best decorations. I still have the three-story architecture plans I created in case I ever have a house built (of course, not to scale and done in colored pencils).

I now had a real-life opportunity to create a home. The number of hours Pandora and I spent on Pinterest, with all the excited conversations about how our life was going to look, are some of my happiest memories.

Today in 2023, everywhere you look there are layouts, floorplans and DIY tips for creating your own tiny house, She Shed or Man Cave. In 2012, there was not so much to go on for inspiration. Tiny homes, RV renovations, and shipping container homes were just gaining popularity. This meant we had to think about every detail of life so we could be efficient with a teeny space as well as comfortable. Three people in a tiny house doesn't give much room for extras. After weeks of brainstorming, the only decision made was the compost toilet had to be behind a door, in the bathroom space which would be a tiled wet room, occupying the back four feet of the container. That was it. No electrical or storage options, just where the toilet had to go.

Calling around to get pricing of electricity, windows, doors, insulation, and plumbing was utterly shocking; some of the costs were as much, if not more than the land had been. Ultimately, we determined it was far more cost effective to buy a different property that had a housing structure on it. Building from scratch was way out of our budget. We started looking again.

We were searching in a small neighborhood that was just north of the southernmost tip of Lake Okeechobee. As you drive down the single road to get in or out of the community, the properties toward the front are forty acres or more, so it makes for a pleasant drive in (unless it has been raining and then the cows give off a disturbing odor). Two and a half miles down the winding road, you come upon the volunteer fire station, the local depot where you can purchase miscellaneous items at a premium and authentic Dominican food, and the community mail center. These three buildings make up the hub of where you *might* see neighbors. All properties beyond this point are two-and-a-half-acre parcels. On weekends we made the two-hour drive out to that same middle of nowhere to look for properties.

There was one property that Pandora and I both loved. Maybe we loved it because it was the first decent place we had come across, or maybe we loved it because the idea of a family homestead was so thrilling, it overtook reality. Lovie was not convinced it was the right one and he hesitated on making the offer. However, he failed to mention his concerns to either of us. When the house went under contract before he made the phone call to put our offer in, we were both furious. Not like "oh shucks, that stinks" kind of mad, actually furious, like silent treatment plus no sexy time. His response was, "It was not meant to be." That did not sit well with either of us since we knew this was where we wanted to live and nice houses weren't exactly abundant. Plus, casually and emotionlessly telling a woman (let alone two at the same time) that something is just "not meant to be" and then moving on without even a discussion or an apology probably won't end well.

But it *was* a lesson that we talked about for years afterwards and I still think about that lesson to this day. If something I want does not come to fruition, I remind myself of this story. If we had gotten that property, it would have drastically altered the path I am on. If we had gotten that house, we would not have found the home that fit every check box for all three of us. We wouldn't have met the neighbors which led to the homestead property Lovie and I have now. The Universe (or God or The Divine or whomever you believe in) always puts you exactly where you are supposed to be. Sometimes you have to be patient.

That home that did fit all the check boxes was a three-bedroom, two-bath, manufactured home at a reasonable price. In order to get there, you turned off the paved road onto a dirt road just wide enough for one car to drive down. There was one streetlamp on that "road" but it was constantly burned out, making it extremely dark at night. There was no fence up or gate up around the property, but you knew the flattened grass trail was the driveway. On the right side was a small pond, just large enough for a few fish and possibly an alligator to live. Inside hardwood floors covered the living room but carpet covered the bedrooms—I loved that part. It had good bones, was structurally sound with a homey vibe that brought up a feeling of happiness. With two and a half acres of land cleared and ready for all our fruit trees we'd been collecting, a pole barn, and separate man cave ready to go, we fell in love. The asking price in 2012 was $65,000. I was stunned. That was peanuts compared to my previous house that I had bought with my ex-wife and several hundred thousand below the starting price in South Florida. This was it. After months of searching, we found our home.

There were hundreds of hurdles we had to jump in order to get financing on a mobile home, it was way harder than I thought it would be. To this day it blows my mind that it is easier to buy a $100,000 car than it is a piece of property half that price. Lovie had no paper trail and bad credit, so he was out for being able to qualify for a loan. Pandora had the income but her credit was bad, so she was not an option to be on a loan either. I was the only one who had both income and credit. The three of us made a business deal within the romantic relationship. I would buy the house in my name, we would all pay for it, and when it was paid off, I would sign it over to their LLC. In all the conversations we had, it just made sense.

Was this a risky move? Yes. But it was one I was willing to take because it meant we could own a house together for the betterment of the family. I knew that the amount of the mortgage was something I could cover on my own if necessary, and I had to be important to the family. I needed to be needed. I needed a purpose in our dynamic and this was a way I could ensure everyone's future. Yes, it was risky. Yes, everyone—I mean everyone—told me it was a terrible idea. No, I did not listen. Most importantly, no, it was not impulsive. I knew what I was getting myself into.

In September of 2012, we closed on that very house for $42,000. The story of how we got it for $20,000 under list price is a fun one to tell. Lovie attended a Robert Allen financial course in the early 2000s. One of the lessons he took to heart about real estate was if you're not embarrassed to make the offer, it's not low enough. When I submitted the contract, it was for an offer of $40,000 ($15,000 below asking). After some back and forth, a price was agreed on, the appraisal came in, and $42,000 is what we paid. I was in awe that I had been able to provide my family with beautiful property with two and a half acres for that price; the house I still owned with my ex-wife was around $150,000.

It never crossed my mind that this was *my* house just because it was in my name. We were all there together at the closing table, we all paid monthly into the mortgage, and we all acknowledged we were in this together. It was OUR home. I was thrilled that I had been able to provide a piece of paradise for our family. I viewed this as evidence that we were all in it for the long haul. They had gotten engaged, but we had all gone to look at a ring for her together, so I was part of the planning now. Plus no one ever makes big financial decisions thinking there is a short term.

The actual purchasing of the house turned out to be the easy part. Next came the interior design.

I was raised in a middle-upper-class family where neutral colors prevailed with just a splash of color. Each room looked like something out of *Southern Living* magazine (changing of course with the times). We had a deep merlot-colored dining room that was far more dramatic than any other color schemes, as the rest of the walls were painted in some shade of white or beige. Throw pillows, paintings, and rugs brought each room together. Bathrooms were the exception, wallpaper was acceptable. I don't recall all of our homes, as there were many over eighteen years living with my parents, but the magnolia powder room in Atlanta stands out the most.

Early on in our childhood, we had an entire basement that made up the playroom for all of our toys, books, and all the shit kids require to be entertained. It was decorated in bright primary colors and had framed Disney posters covering the walls. As we grew up, we were allowed to paint an accent wall in the bedroom (I had a bright purple wall in the mid-nineties that all my friends were jealous of) or have fun wallpaper that ran underneath the chair railing. In my high-school years, Mama allowed me to wallpaper below the chair railing in a loud leopard print— it was incredible and on-brand with my animal-print-everything obsession that lasted into my early twenties.

In our new home, Pandora took the lead. I observed that island culture's relished a more colorful theme throughout the entire house. Bright walls, each painted a different color, and patterned dishes. Thick fabrics on ornate sofas, with heavy lamps and lots of browns and gold. Everything is large and regal.

We moved all her furniture from the Hollywood house, as all of mine was stored in PODS in Orlando until further no-tice, into the new Farmhouse. When it came time to pick wall colors, there was a vast contradiction of options on what was desirable for a home. I was in favor of neutral colors, whites, and grays. Pandora was in favor of different shades of yellows and oranges on all the walls. Can you guess who won that debate?

The wallpapered living room was painted a sunny shade of yellow, with an accent wall of bright yellow-orange. I was not impressed at all. This was so not how I wanted our house to look. Our views of what looked good were just different, but I was a good girl and just went with the flow. At the end of the day, these things were just cosmetic and would not affect the fundamentals of our relationship; I resented them nonetheless. Over time, I stopped noticing, and it all became familiar.

On the other side of the spectrum was Lovie's choice of how to decorate our bedroom. It was again, not what I wanted, but I was more okay with it because it was not totally the opposite of what I like, right colors-wrong theme. What Pandora picked was opposite of my ideals of classy and everything was her style. There was no compromise, nothing represented me in the main space. What Lovie wanted was also more okay with me because he rarely weighed in on decorating and when he did, I knew it really meant something. Luckily, Pandora and I wanted to make Lovie happy, so the decision on how to decorate the bedroom and bathroom was up to him.

We went with a black and white master bedroom and bathroom. The bedroom had all white walls with black vinyl stickers on one, mirrored closet doors on another, and three large mirrors covering each of the other two walls. I tend to find vinyl stickers on walls tacky, but it was a vast improvement over the living room colors. And yes, I just said vinyl stickers are tacky and skipped over the three-mirrored-walls part—everyone loves mirrors. The carpet we had installed was solid black, low-pile and actually looked pretty cool once it was in. We set up Bed Island so we'd have ample space to sleep, despite the fact that we were always cuddling up next to each other. The makeshift bed required two sets of sheets and two large blankets to accommodate the oversized space. Being the only piece of furniture in that room, it was THE focal point. In the beginning, none of the bedding matched because we had more important things to spend our money on. Eventually, we brought my king mattress down from Orlando so that the bedding would look more cohesive.

The master bathroom was the quintessential mobile home norm. Wallpaper, tan flooring, large corner garden tub and stand-up shower with light wood cabinets and beige counter-tops. That HAD to go. We painted the cabinets and counter-tops white, painted over the wallpaper with white and black accents, and laid down black tile flooring. Black and white tiles to be exact, not my jam, but it didn't suck.

One of the spare bedrooms was turned into a library. It was my favorite room in the house. The other bedroom was the one space I got to decorate anyway I wanted. The scrapbook room was painted a baby blue and covered with folding tables displaying punches, containers four shelves high busting out with stickers, thick binders of completed memory books, and all the crafting things. This is also the room that held my closet. While we shared the bedroom, the master closet was not big enough for three people.

When Pandora told me I would be using the scrapbook room closet, I felt ousted. Questions like, "Should I read into this?" "Am I being separated on purpose?" "Is this leading to me having a separate room?" "Why can't you use that closet so it all feels like shared space?" These were all valid questions in the moment but once I had time to process the actual logistics, it made sense. I was no less included just because I walked across the living room to my closet; I have a ton of clothes. Eventually, I took over the guest bathroom as well. It just made sense—I love to have my lotions and makeup displayed out.

Outside of decorating the house, life with two females in the same domain was relatively easy. We had established a routine at the Hollywood house that easily transitioned to The

Farm. I never questioned who was in charge and spoke up only when I felt passionately about something. To my surprise, she was more open-minded about what I had to say once we officially lived together, more than she was at the Hollywood house. I attributed this to her being more accepting of our new family status and the permanency that owning a house together implied. Deep down I had a nagging feeling it was more about pacifying me since I was the sole owner of the property, but negative thoughts breed negative outcomes. I chose to see that my opinion was requested in most decisions.

Our life those first few months at The Farm was exactly what I had wished for. We decided what would be done on the property by having family decisions where we all laid out our individual options and then found the best compromise possible over candles and wine. Money was paid out in three equal amounts when we purchased anything, and individual budgets were taken into consideration.

When out in public, we all held hands. This, for us, showed each other the solidarity in the life we were creating together. Couples hold hands all the time, why couldn't our throuple? There were glances here and there, but in general, most humans are more worried about themselves versus noticing the people around them. For those that did notice, I can only imagine their confusion. Pandora and I would hold hands walking into the Publix grocery store, not strange in South Florida in 2012 to see a lesbian couple. But then you would see Lovie hug and kiss her in the cereal aisle while I was picking out a coffee. Fast-forward to the produce section. You would see Lovie with his hands on my hips, reaching around my midsection to "help" pick out the best apples. If anyone noticed any of this, they would be thoroughly confused to see all three of us joking together standing in line, unloading our buggy, paying the cashier, and once again holding hands on the way out. I must admit, I loved the idea of people not understanding. I believe there is a certain gift in seeing things you don't understand to help yourself grow. It forces the mind to have deeper internal conversations, to see the world differently. Of course, this only applies as long as you do not start out with a negative. A confused mind always says "no."

We called ourselves a family and they were My Honeys. We all had nicknames for each other, Mama, Papa, and Little One. Okay—hindsight, mine might appear to be degrading but it came from a place of love. It signified my place and had an heir of innocence that they saw in me. The total number of dynamics that we had to maintain was a feat in and of itself. In a monogamous scenario you have two relationships to nurture: your partnership and (hopefully) one with yourself. Never forget that building a life with someone, committing yourself to a marriage or multiple relationships does not mean you lose your independence as an individual. If you are not growing as a human being, you won't experience the fullness of life. Partners must grow individually in order to grow together. Will Smith said it best: "You cannot make a person happy. You can make a person smile, you can make a person feel good, you can make a person laugh. But whether or not a person is happy is deeply and totally and utterly out of your control. Every person is responsible for his or her happiness. No one else can do it for you."

That, my friends, is way easier said than done. I had a difficult time balancing the four dynamics plus my own journey, especially my weight journey. For starters, there was the central relationship of the three of us. Let's pause right here. I mean to say, this *should* be the central part of our dynamic. Two out of our three agreed. However, one person saw the triangle as a secondary act, an ancillary piece of the puzzle. This could be the ultimate downfall right from the get-go. Everyone must be on the same page, just as with any type of relationship. Without it, there is no way to succeed long term. Oh sure, you can surf the highs and lows for years, but eventually, everything will crash and burn because the core goal of partners is different. If one piece of a puzzle is missing, it will never be complete.

Within our triangle of love, there were three additional relationships: me and Pandora, Lovie and Pandora, and Lovie and me. Pandora saw her and Lovie as the central core of the triangle (instead of the three of us being the core).

To be clear, she did not hide this viewpoint. I agreed and verbalized that I was on board for this dynamic. My recollection of this may sound jaded and preachy. I am in a far different place than I was then and I am not sure how to place myself back in that mindset now that I have grown more confident and recognize my worth as a partner. Nevertheless, I didn't know any better and thought this was how it was supposed to work. That is why I am choosing to write this for others. There is no way it is "supposed" to be.

With the two of them being at the core, that left a need for definition in the relationship between me and her as well as Lovie and me. There was no room for confusion here. She and I were in a romantic relationship and the three of us were together as long as she was the primary, but there was NO romantic relationship between him and me as far as she was concerned. Period. It was a "V" shape for her. I wanted to be a family. I loved her. I was in love with her. I also loved him.

The "V" dynamic is a well-known one in the ethical non-monogamy world. It is not uncommon for one partner to be the point person and have two partners that know about each other and consent to share. There is also the possibility that a "V" can be considered a family, even if the other two partners do not have a romantic or sexual relationship. That is how she wanted it structured. However, that wasn't what she proposed in discussions. When she talked about us, it was "family" but when she talked about Lovie and me, it was NOT boyfriend/girlfriend. That part was crystal clear but there was never further discussion on what he and I actually were to each other. Were we the tips of the V? Since we were sexually involved, it got into a gray area.

As there was no clear definition, both Lovie and I considered ourselves equal partners who were in a romantic relationship; we just didn't verbalize that label to her to keep the peace until she became more comfortable. We chose to act that way without clarification. We had conversations about the way we felt about each other. Not the most honest approach, but it seemed to be the only option at the time because both of us believed she wanted a lifelong poly relationship in the end.

For six months we lived in loving bliss. The farm was coming along. We all contributed in different ways to help create a paradise to thrive in. Lovie worked outside ten hours a day while Pandora made sure everyone was hydrated and fed at all times. We constructed a fence around two and a half acres by hand, with her and I taking turns using posthole diggers until our shoulders burned, then giving them back to him. We raised chickens, rabbits and goats, we planted sixty-five fruit trees, and we had various herb and vegetable gardens going. Most of all, we all three were happy and content.

We celebrated holidays together. Christmas of 2012, we baked cookies on December 24 and laid out cookies for Santa. I surprised them by stuffing stockings in the middle of the night and we woke up to find Lovie had snuck out to eat the cookies as if St. Nick had in fact visited. On Valentine's Day 2013, we had a quiet dinner at home with a small cake and bottle of wine, super classy and romantic. We toasted each other standing around the kitchen island, taking turns professing things we loved about each other. These are two of my favorite memories. Our home was filled with love, appreciation, and wonderment.

We had a nightly routine where we would all shower and do our own routines, then wind down snuggled on the wraparound sofa to watch a movie and go to bed together at the same time. If someone wasn't tired yet, you just played on your phone or read a book. It really was paradise. It wasn't nights filled with debauchery or constant escapades. It was just two women and one man building a life together based on love and shared goals.

During those months, it was always a letdown when work got in the way. I was still traveling quite a bit around the Southeast and travel times were even longer now that we lived in the middle of nowhere; my twenty-minute trip to the airport was now two hours.

On one hand, I loved being gone because I had time to socialize with friends and catch up with phone calls. On the other hand, my FOMO was intense. I missed our routines. I had to know what was happening every minute of every day on the farm and that struck a chord with Pandora. She would ask me why I always asked what they were doing. Every phone call started with "what are y'all up to?" She started to question my motive when I wanted a full rundown of the day. I genuinely was interested in each single event that happened but it must have come across as suspicious, I guess? It killed me not being involved.

There was no way to explain why it was so important to me to know all the play-by-play details, but I guess that it's a fundamental, primal need to feel connected to the people I'm in love with. I didn't want to feel left behind. Many small events can lead to large change. It is not limited to home life either. There is a certain bond that people who share any space on a daily basis create.

If you share an office or a cubicle with someone, you have created routines and if something changes, it throws off the vibe. When you share a home, there is someone who cooks, someone who cleans, specific spots on the sofa, the activities of day-to-day life are set. To really appreciate the bond that is created in each space of your life, for the next three days, pay attention to the mundane conversations that you have with your partner or office buddies. You will notice that plans are made, decisions discussed that you would never consider "important" but they will add up to building blocks of your life.

They may be boring or small, but still blocks.

On top of the heavy work-travel schedule, I was also coordinating family and friend visits over the weekends; my cup was super full. It was a tricky schedule to balance, but it made the time I was home seem more precious and appreciated by all parties. Pandora once told me I was the life of the party; it was always an adventure when I was home. The only thing sweeter to me was hearing, "I love you." My role had been officially defined: I was the one who brought laughter and excitement.

I held onto that statement like a mantra. I became more bubbly on the phone. I made sure to plan fun events and excursions. I would come home with fiesta decorations, tequila, and chips for Taco and Tequila night. I made signs to put around hotel rooms when they came to meet me. We had picnics and luaus. I'd pick up pizza and season-themed plates on my way home. The Dollar Tree has every item needed for a party, and I am convinced I keep them in business.

Balance is important though. There were issues that went unaddressed in order for me to stay fun, things I wanted to talk about or feelings I had but would not talk about because they were serious. There were occasions where awkward or uncomfortable vibes were present when I'd get home. I hoped they were just between Pandora and Lovie, issues I was not involved in. Frequently, there were tensions between them but as part of our family code, we tried to keep tiffs between only two of us separate. I tried not to overanalyze these feelings.

It is normal for any relationship, whether monogamous or poly, for partners to get annoyed with each other or have mild disagreements. This is not a sign of weakness. It means you're comfortable enough with each other to freely express emotions, but should also have respect for each other to step away before things are said or done that cannot be undone. Words cut deeper than any object. An argument does not have to be addressed immediately. You can ask for time to process and come back to it later. Just make sure you actually come back to it when calmer heads can prevail.

Whenever this happened, I tended to side more with Pandora for two reasons. Most importantly, it was so that she knew I loved her, that I was committed to her and that she could count on me. I would not turn on her when there was any inclination of siding with him. I did not want her to think I would be the kind of person who would use their fight to bring him and me closer, so I made myself extra clingy to her. I never thought about how that might be perceived but it seemed like a way for me to prove loyalty when there were still questions in her mind. The second reason was because he could be unpleasant to be around when he got in one of his moods after a repetitive argument between them. His frustration level was not containable. I didn't want to be included in his anger, so I steered clear of him.

At the end of May 2013, Pandora and I celebrated our one-year anniversary of when I moved into the Hollywood house by going to Vegas. We knew we wanted to do something with just me and her for a long weekend but could not decide between New York or Vegas. Since New York was about five times more expensive, Vegas won. She had never flown first class. Gift-giving is my primary love language, so I paid for round-trip tickets for us. I felt like such a baller. It was important to me to give her that experience. We both were nervous, even if she said it in a sarcastic way. Spending time, just us, without Lovie to use as a buffer was not something we did often. By buffer, I mean, at any time we could bring him into the conversation, or we would all still go to sleep together after having a "just girls'" day.

We flew out on Thursday morning from South Florida and, even with the three-hour time change, didn't get to the hotel until early evening. There were flight delays, an unexpected landing to refuel, and the longest taxi line I had ever seen. That is saying something since I averaged over sixty flights per year. By the time we got to The Palms resort, it was room service and bed. The Palms resort was labeled as a "budget hotel" just off the strip but had been recently renovated to appeal to more people. Even the "budget" room was over $300 per night. My first shock of Vegas: no coffee makers in the room. Every morning I went to go play $5 blackjack to get free coffee and Baileys. I drink my coffee black, but who could resist free alcohol? Not me.

Friday and Saturday, we spent just walking the strip, exploring different hotels, and attending a time-share presentation that promised free show tickets and $100 in casino cash in old Las Vegas. If you have never been to a time-share presentation, don't. They make it sound so affordable that we *almost* texted Lovie about buying one. Lucky for us, the agent was so stunned when we told him we had to speak to our husband that we got off easy.

Vegas is known for its phenomenal shows, so naturally we took in two. Absinthe, which was incredibly mind-blowing not only for the spectacle of tricks and talent but also the raunchy, racist, and stereotypical interaction with the audience. I was terrified we were going to be singled out. A mixed-race lesbian couple, every naughty MC's dream. Sitting in the second-to-last row of a tiny theater did not offer much protection. Every time the ringmaster turned toward us, I sank in my seat. Being picked out of a crowd was my worst nightmare. Saturday night we attended my first topless burlesque show, aptly titled, X Burlesque. It was ... underwhelming. To be fair, it is hard for a show to top the thrill of going to a swingers club. Neither night ended in grand parties or any typical Vegas shenanigans. A couple of quarters here and there in flashy machines and then back to the hotel for bed. Even three hours behind, in the city that parties twenty-four hours a day, Pandora was set on regularly scheduled bedtimes.

Our last day, Sunday, we enjoyed what the hotel had to offer, starting with a champagne brunch buffet. Those three words in order are pure magic. Brunch is the most wonderful meal created by humans. Champagne and bacon?! I will drive miles just to enjoy this simple pleasure in life. After we stuffed ourselves, we finally made an appearance at the pool that was covered with beautiful people.

That was short-lived. Pandora doesn't do sun, and I felt like a walrus. We then spent some time apart, which I had zero recollection of until I read my brief journal notes from that weekend. I didn't seem to find that strange according to what I journaled. 2023 me finds that very odd. On a romantic anniversary weekend, just the two of us, for three days, we needed alone time. It had been forty-eight hours. Red flag number one missed.

Once we were back together in the room, we finally had sex. I enjoyed it and thought it was amazing, but I got the impression she did not. I felt weird and incredibly awkward about it. Those feelings were not what I was hoping for from that experience. Red flag number two missed. All in all, this trip made me feel like we got closer on a deeper emotional level. It was less about sexy time and more about building a long-term connection. Holding her and cuddling in bed each night meant the world to my heart but I couldn't help feeling like I wasn't enough.

Once back home, we picked up all the same routines as before. I did feel closer and thought this trip put her and me on a similar page about everything. How could we not be? We had many, *many* intense conversations in Vegas. We should be all straight now. I love her. I love our family. I am here for the long haul.

The summer of 2013 played out like a bipolar character who was off their meds. One minute from her was "I love you," "I miss you," and "I can't wait until you get home." Then I would get home and it was passive-aggressive everything. I looked at her wrong. I looked at him wrong. I stayed in bed too long. The list was unlistable.

It all came to a head on June 23, 2013.

I wish I could remember the buildup to one specific conversation. Did I say something that upset her? Did she seem anxious or uncomfortable about something? All I remember is sitting on the arm of the brown leather sofa, my feet planted on the floor, and her taking my hand, sitting with her legs tucked underneath her. Her beautiful face definitely had "something's wrong" written on it. Lovie had been weird after I got home but he has a way to make you feel out of sorts after a disagreement with him, so I assumed she wanted to vent about a conversation they'd had. As soon as she started the conversation, I knew it was bad. I do not recall the exact sequence of words she used, so here is what I have written in my journals as words or phrases that I found significant.

"Little One, I only want you to be home once every two weeks. When you are gone less than that, Papa and I haven't had time to reconnect. I need more time to work on myself as well."

My face was frozen trying to decide if I should respond. My heart started pounding so loudly inside my chest I feared she could hear it. I wanted to play it cool but could feel my face getting red and I started to sweat. I'm sorry—did I just hear that correctly?? My girlfriend just asked me to stay away from *our* home for at least two weeks every time I left so that they can reconnect?? My presence created *such* a disruption between them that she doesn't want me to come back to the place we *all* share, where *all* my belongings are, more than every fourteen days? I was flabbergasted. The hurt manifested physically. Never in my life could I have imagined someone telling me that I could not return to what was supposed to be my sanctuary until an "approved" time.

I spent the majority of that weekend in the shower, crying. I didn't want her to see me so upset. I felt pathetic.

I deserved so much more in love, yet I was willing to honor this request?

It is an unbelievably selfish request.

Do I want to be in a relationship with someone who would ask me to do this?

It is not my fault she can't function and get her shit together when I am gone, so why am I the one being punished?

She put blame on me for things beyond my control.

She gaslights me into believing I am the problem.

What is wrong with me? Her words have contradictions in each sentence. I'm confused, and I can't keep up.

I'm tired of being a gypsy. I want a home.

I want stability and some semblance of a routine.

Is this what love should feel like?

Of course, I am in camp "what-the-fuck-did-my-girlfriend-just-say-to-me" but if I am being objective, this had to be a tough conversation for her as well. I can only guess what was going through her mind. There was a calculated risk in this type of conversation. What would happen if I actually fought back? What if I decided to bring Lovie into the conversation and ask if he felt this way too?

In order for her to sit straight faced in front of someone whom she loved and just flat out tell them to not come home but every fourteen days, she must have been feeling some awful sort of way. What was she not getting from him while I was gone that she so desperately needed? What type of hellish narrative was going on in her head that tormented her into thinking I was a threat to their relationship? How much time did she agonize over the right way to say these things to me? Girl brain can be a real bitch and if you lose touch with objectiveness, ever, for a split second, all hell breaks loose. She lost herself in a narrative she believed in and was grabbing hold the only way she knew how: Manipulate the one who causes the insecurity. My fingers just typed that out on their own and I will choose to leave it—manipulation is a heavy word. How I intended to say that was that she felt the only way to change how things were going was to adjust the frequency of time spent with whom she felt was the issue, me. Less me equaled more them.

I know it sounds childish, but I was fuming that Lovie did not catch any of this brunt. He didn't have to deal with this type of treatment. She never said things like this to him. She never talked down to him. In fact, she hid her feelings from him. Years later, I asked him about this conversation because it was such a painful part of our story. He claimed to have no idea what I was talking about, that he had zero knowledge that she spoke to me about this. According to him, she never discussed this proposal with him, and she never mentioned that she had talked with me about staying gone so they could reconnect. It is a hard pill to swallow, that he was completely clueless to this. That she was able to keep her feelings about me being in our home from him is a far-fetched concept, since I was under the impression they talked about *everything*. I chose to believe him since it's in the past now but I will never actually know. Sometimes it really is better to let bygones be bygones.

Hobbling along the rest of the summer was exhausting for both of us. I was doing my best to pacify her request, which meant even more travel than I was already doing. Trying to smile and convince family that everything was peachy at home was emotionally draining. At home, each quick turn of emotion and being mentally beat down were taking its toll. By mid-July, Pandora decided she wanted to go visit a friend in Texas. She needed a break. The breaking point for her had come. Our dynamic was not what she wanted, but she needed time alone to figure out the logistics.

Her ticket was booked and she was leaving on August 1 for two weeks. Since we had to go to Fort Lauderdale anyway to take her to the airport, we took advantage and celebrated my birthday the day before in a hotel. All three of us were in a somber type of mood but I felt myself having hope that we would make it past this storm when I opened my birthday gift. Relationships have ebbs and flows, you have to ride them out to be successful. With the sheer amount of communication I thought we had, I knew we would make it through this.

To this day, it is still one of the most thoughtful and sentimental gifts I have ever received. They (I know it was really her and they both got credit for it) picked out a clear glass bottle that looked as if a genie should live in it, and three different containers filled with colored sand. Each color was to represent us as a family; black for Lovie, pink for Pandora, and blue for me. We each poured a layer of sand in individually to represent our own life path and contributions. The remainder of the bottle was filled by all three of us pouring our representative color in at the same time so it all was mixed together. The thought alone brought tears to my eyes. When we all poured in at the same time, it felt like a spiritual ceremony that really connected us. All the drama of the last few months suddenly appeared to mean the worst was over. She was all in now.

Two weeks turned into a month. A month turned into two months. She left us for two months and it was a nonstop roller coaster. She was scheduled to originally return around their two-year anniversary, but she extended her trip for the first time saying she was not ready to come home yet. Being the fixer that I am and being that I love anniversaries, I kept telling him to send her flowers in Texas. Being the frugal mongrel he is, he did not want to. Eventually, he came around and asked what he should write on the card. Since they already referred to each other as husband and wife (despite not being married or having any plans to do so in the near future), I told him to say something along the lines of, "Happy Anniversary, Mrs. Jolicoeur. I love you." To me, this was a genius plan because the flowers would arrive before the actual anniversary, which meant he put forethought in. I thought this would make her smile and feel loved knowing that he had thought about their day in advance.

This backfired on me. Not on him but on me. I got in trouble because she did not like the gesture. I got in trouble again because he and I had sex on their anniversary. Woke up, not a clue what day of the week it was because neither of us are morning people, had sex, and went about our day. We had been alone for two weeks and given "permission" to do so.

From that point on, she clung to that single event as proof I was the issue. Her phone conversations with me were shorter and she did not have any sweet responses. I loved her. She was working on herself.

She finally came home two weeks into September. I was exhausted from what I saw as nonsense. You don't just leave a relationship to be dramatic. Lovie and I had conversations that, at this point in time, it was us and she could either take it or leave it. We were done with the drama. Being gone and pouting like a child for one and a half months was a little over-kill.

That resolve quickly changed for him as soon as she stepped off that plane thirty pounds skinnier and beautiful as ever.

CHAPTER 8

BREAKING UP IS HARD TO DO – AGAIN

"What we perceive as limitations have the potential to become strengths greater than what we had when we were 'normal' or unbroken ... when something breaks, something greater often emerges from the cracks."
— Nnedi Okorafor —

I will never forget that morning in late September, just a week after she had come home. I can't say that it came out of no-where, clearly it did not. I had a dream while she was gone about her breaking up with me. Her awkward non-response when I told her about it on the phone was unsettling.

Pandora had only been back from her hiatus to Texas a week, and everything was super strained. I figured if things were going to be fine, she would have been happy to see me, want to hold me, but she didn't. She had lost weight and was looking thin. There was a phone conversation where she told me that she'd lost five pounds. Later she said she had only said five pounds because she knew I would lose equal amounts to be in "competition" with her. What? Competition? I thought we were partners who wanted to support each other, cheer each other on and lose weight together. Apparently not.

What did shock me this fateful September morning were

the words that came out of Lovie's mouth. That I did not see coming.

Everything she did to try and keep me and Lovie from getting too close, even from Texas, had failed. In fairness to her, nothing between me and him actually changed. We were still the same partners who loved each other the same way as we had in the beginning of our triad. She never wanted to acknowledge this. She just got more upset about everything happening at home, every action, and each mundane day-to-day task. By the second or third time she extended her trip, he was frustrated and over (his words) "her drama." I was too. I wanted to scream at her that she is the one who left us for over a month. She was the one who kept choosing to stay longer. She was the one being unreasonable and changing the rules. But I never did say those things. I did not want to rock the fragile boat, so I apologized to her and bitched about it to him. Not a healthy choice but a valuable life lesson I would pull from later. I also knew that no matter what he said, he did love her more. He wouldn't walk away from her. Knowing that, I was still blindsided by his words.

We were outside for our morning smoke, and she came out with us, something she never did. It was a sunny day and there were still some late mangos on the tree that was five feet from the edge of my sitting area. They sat inside the man cave and I was sitting in my usual chair on the porch just outside the screen window. I don't recall how the conversation started. I just remember him saying these words while she stayed silent.

"We think we will be stronger just the two of us."

Wait, what? WE? WE was him and me just one week earlier making the decision things needed to change and wanted to open up the restrictions she put on us. If she said no, then we would cross that bridge. WE had discussed our future, both with and without her in it based on her decision to stay with us or not. WE were finally in a place that we were happy for a month consecutively with no drama and WE were falling more in love. WE discussed all the possibilities of what we would accomplish and dreams we wanted to create.

Just like that, WE had nothing to do with me. I was out. It didn't seem real. My heart was being used as a dartboard; every statement was another dart being plunged deeper into my soul until I could not take anymore.

He talked at me for an hour, maybe it was longer or maybe it was shorter, time seemed to stop. I was chain-smoking, trying to keep the tears from turning into a waterfall. Don't let them see weakness. She didn't say anything, just sat there next to him alternating between looking at the floor with the occasional glance up at me. This was the first and only time I saw her cower in a situation. I asked questions, wanting answers that he couldn't give, and she wouldn't give. I was now out of the family, and it was not up for discussion. I was no longer in the love circle. Once again, my body was cringed up from learning I had been wrong. I just focused on the last mangos hanging off the tree.

The thoughts ruminating in my brain ranged from where am I going to live to how to can I explain this to everyone? I'd tried so hard to make my world look "normal." It had only been a year and I still solely owned the property. What was the next move there?

Later that morning, while we were headed into Fort Lauderdale (we were going down several days a week for work) I called my mom within minutes of leaving the farm, kind of a risky move. My parents and I were in the don't-ask-don't-tell phase (and we still are to a degree). I was bawling, like the ugly cry, where your face is barely recognizable, snot is flowing at a pace that you cannot keep up with, and your words are barely comprehensible.

"We broke up. It's so hard to balance all these different dynamics. I don't know what to do. Where will I live? I don't know how to handle this. I don't know if I can start over again"

My mom was a champ. I knew that day that my mom loved me unconditionally. She did not ask any questions, she listened, and kept repeating,

"I'm so sorry, honey."

"I wish I could make this better for you."

"I wish I could take the pain away."

"You will be okay."

She did not seem to flinch while I blurted out all my poly laundry that had never been said openly before.

It didn't feel like I'd be okay, but I knew deep down she was right. I had started over before and I would do it again. You never know what might happen in the future.

PS: When I said I was thinking about "what the future might hold," that's code for "I don't believe that he wants to break up, I think he and I will work it out." I was 1000 percent convinced that she was the only one who wanted this breakup because she was jealous of me. She never considered me an equal partner, nor did she want me to be an equal, so I had to go. Spoiler alert: turned out he *did* want to make it work with her and willingly agreed to end it with me under the condition that they find a new partner for a wife potential. That was the key point in getting his agreeance on my exile.

As time progressed though, he learned a hard lesson. He couldn't completely cut me out because his heart still wanted me. Jealousy and insecurity *were* the reasons Pandora wanted the breakup. But despite her promise, she never had the intention of adding a third person. She wanted to be the one and only wife/woman in his life with any consistency.

For those of you new to this ... that is not polyamory, that is monogamy with a swinging spice. I get one question at this part in our history: Why would I want to make it work with a man who had me as second choice?

The first reason: I looked at his decision to stay with her the same way I view parents who stay together just for the kids; there is too much at stake to split up right then. They want to fix something that's broken. Best case, things work out. Worst case, everyone is miserable for a couple of years, but at least they gave it a go. Life moves on. He was in love with her plus had fifteen years' friendship. There was a mortgaged house, a business, and a lifelong dream of farming entangled with her. He had to try to make it work.

The second part is in the perspective. Yes, I could have said, "You chose me as second," "You came back when you realized the grass wasn't greener," or "You made your choice, blah blah blah." We both had learning and growing to do during this era. Without our different experiences, we wouldn't be the humans we are today. Going through those trials individually taught us both different things. Now, neither of us takes for granted the small things like we did before.

The next several weeks in the house were an emotional roller coaster. From acting that I was excited for my next chapter to crying as quietly as possible in the shower for extended amounts of time. The end was here, but we had to live together until I moved into my new apartment. Not awkward at all. The three of us tried to act normally, almost to a fault.

I was moving out at the end of October. All of our lives were changing dramatically but we acted like nothing was wrong. We made dinner together, watched movies before going to the bed we still shared, and spoke more lovingly than we had in weeks, most of the time. Lovie and Pandora even went with me to look at houses and apartments. When I found the best option, it was a group decision. Clearly boundaries were not my strong suit.

They would talk about the farm. Occasionally I forgot I was no longer a part of decisions, until I was smacked with a weight-being-hurled-at-my-chest sensation that came as my brain sent a red-alert reminder: I wasn't included.

Something I never forgot: We bought the property together (in my name solely), we all paid equally to make upgrades and improvements, and we all put sweat equity into it.

Bitter, party of one.

I was jaded, obviously, but she seemed to say or do small things with malicious intentions. Mostly tiny little stabs like talking about vacations, holidays, and even lifestyle events while I was in the conversation. Yes, I still lived there for the time, but I was gone an awful lot for her not to have been able to find better moments to discuss these things, like during the week while I was traveling. There were signs I'd ignored about her character, but this was a new level of mean that opened my eyes just a tiny bit more. Objectively, my heart had been broken so it's possible I was misinterpreting her actions or motives. Then again, sometimes things really are exactly what they seem.

The silver lining during this time was a trip to Seattle after "the conversation." I was sinking into a depression and needed my sisters, who both lived in Washington state. Nothing offers a fresh perspective like flying 3,500 miles to the farthest possible place in the contiguous US. South Florida's heat and humidity can make you feel sticky and stagnant, like your problems just hover around you. There's something comforting in the overcast days of Seattle, with its gray skies and cold wind. The crispness in the breeze and constant drizzle reminds me of fresh starts. Every time you go outside, you're being cleansed of burdens. There is an energy in Seattle unlike any other city, it calms me. And if that wasn't enough to start healing me, it's also filled with my favorite medicines for sadness: abundance of retail therapy, lots of drinking in unique restaurants, and snuggles with my nieces.

I spent that long weekend at KT's, my middle sister, and we took a day trip to Anacortes Island for a whale-watching tour. I am a huge lover of orcas; I'll nerd out telling you fun facts for an hour if you sit still long enough to listen. Seeing them in the wild has been a bucket list dream since I first saw Shamu at SeaWorld, but as you can imagine, there are not many orcas off the coasts of Florida. When she suggested this adventure,

I forgot about my life back in South Florida the entire day. I was present as we drove up the coastline, watching the dark green evergreen forest rush by, taking in the quaint towns and their vibrantly colored trees with changing leaves, wondering what life would be like here. According to the calendar, it was fall. According to the thermometer, we needed full winter gear for our four-hour search to see whales. I was only saved from frostbite by the many, many layers I piled on. The wind was wickedly brutal as we sped across the water.

All the freezing sleet in my face was worth it at that first glimpse. We saw orcas. It was such a peaceful, magical moment in my life. The way they move their massive bodies calmly through the water, seeing the family pod interact is mesmerizing to me. I had a strong connection to nature and sharing that experience with my sister amplified my healing.

This single event did not change the course my life, it didn't change the pain I was going through. However, it did coat my heart with a memory that I think about more than anything else during those months. I don't associate this trip with negative happening in my life to take me there, this trip stands as its own positive moment in time. I got to spend time, just me and my sis, crossing off one of my bucket list items, in one of the most beautiful places on earth.

Once I got back home, time both stood still and time flew starting with that day in September until the end of October. It was agony watching the calendar as days expired. I needed to hold each day because it was getting closer to the last. We were happier than we had been in several months and I just wanted time to slow down. Eventually, there was no more time and moving day came.

I was making more money than ever in my career and was able to look at all areas of South Florida since budget restrictions were more lenient now. Fort Lauderdale Beach was my first choice. The beach has always been my happy place, the ocean my grounding zone. I figured the best place to heal was living right there, at the ocean. We made appointments to tour several different places, one in particular made it as the top contender.

It was a sea-foam green, concrete bungalow that stood bundled around several other small houses that were built in the '60's or '70s. The inside had two bedrooms, one bathroom, one closet and was extremely old and outdated, not in a charming way either. But it was four houses up from the boardwalk which meant I would be able to walk to the beach in less than one minute. The ad said I could see the beach from standing outside the front door which was kind of a stretch but not totally inaccurate. The only downside of my dream house (other than one closet), it was $1600 a month *plus* utilities and not in the best part of town.

It wasn't a bad area per se but with older windows and doors, and with me living alone in a single-story house, and being directly off A1A, my confidence level wasn't at a ten. After the Orlando break-ins, the safety factor was top priority. I also had flashbacks to my time in my fancy high-rise apartment in downtown Orlando. Prime location, lots to do, paying beaucoup bucks and yet I never went anywhere because I was healing from a heartache involving the three of us. It was deja vu. No matter how much I want to be a sleek city chick, I am a country lady or least a suburb girl. I passed on the beach house.

Other appointments were at apartments and single rooms to rent (those are a hard pass for me). Fort Lauderdale Beach, Sunrise, West Palm and Boynton Beach were all lovely areas, but I had to go with my gut—I wanted to be around places I knew. Some people like completely fresh starts. I needed a jump-start by having familiarity.

I landed in a cute two-bedroom apartment with a second-floor patio overlooking a small side road lined with trees. It was a massive apartment community, but I was in a small building, right by the back entrance gate and it was quiet. Best part, it was only $1100 per month. One of the main reasons I picked this place was because it was in the middle of all my favorite places: the mall, Barnes and Noble, Ross, TJ Maxx, Walmart, Starbucks, Whole Foods, Publix, plus all my other favorite restaurants. My new paradise. It was close enough to where Lovie and Pandora stayed when in town, but far enough so it didn't look suspicious, about a fifteen-minute drive. I know, I know, we broke up but since they helped me find my new place and even had input on my new mattress and furniture, I had some hopes. Be far enough away, close enough as well.

I got settled in surprisingly fast. I could've easily flown anywhere to trade emotions for work, but there was a moment I decided to just be still. I could be more than this submissive, sad person who was waiting around for crumbs to drop. It was not a major epiphany; it was a moment I thought: Huh ... I can do anything I want. Why didn't I do it before?

I scheduled more time home instead of running away. I tried new activities like reading an actual book in my incredibly buttery-soft new recliner. Audibles were all I'd had on deck for the last four years so reading was an old habit turned new again. That recliner was too great for just reading in, so I started cross-stitching again so I could spend more time snuggled in it. And don't laugh, cross-stitching is very cool.

I started working with a life coach out of Seattle. She asked hard questions that I did not want to answer. Somehow, she got me there and I didn't mind the homework assignments she gave me. I got cable for the first time in five years. I attempted recipes and tried to be more adventurous in the kitchen. This venture was hit or miss. Thirty-nine years of my life so far and no one has ever accused me of being a wiz in the kitchen. The bar, yes, but nothing involving an oven.

There was a small, Asian restaurant that I could walk to and eat at several times a week. Always the same thing: miso soup, salad with ginger dressing, and a vegetable roll. I really enjoyed the independence and solitude. I had the ability to make decisions on what I could and couldn't do before but there were others' feelings to consider. This was just me, myself, and I to think about.

For the first three months.

Pandora would come over from time to time in those first three months. It was strained and I was unsure of how to act. How should I greet her at the door? A hug, a kiss, or just a hand gesture to "come on in"? Are we friends who just hang out or can I hold your hand in the car? I wanted to get back together but I could not be too eager since I wanted her to keep coming over.

Lovie rarely came with her in the beginning, his reasons were usually that he had to work or he just didn't want to spend time with me. Harsh and hard to hear but the truth. This was a point that Pandora never missed an opportunity to share with me, he did not WANT to hang out with me. He was the bad guy in the whole thing. "See, it's me that is here, I am the one who wants to be around, I am the good guy. He does not want to be here." I accepted her olive branches in order to get back in good graces, just so I could get back in his good graces. Not an attractive fact but true. A little voice would nag at me that this was a show, just in case she needed me later, so it seemed to be mutually beneficial.

If I had a dollar for every time I have said or thought "hindsight is 20/20," I would be a millionaire. She and I had no business being friends or trying to make a relationship work after I moved out. At that point, neither of us had a true or positive desire for our romance to work. It became toxic for us both.

My theory proved to be correct after those first three months when they started staying with me and eventually moved into my apartment for six months.

Yup ... after all that, the "we are stronger together" bullshit, they ended up moving into my apartment for almost six months. How did that happen? Why did I allow this? What caused her to change her mind? These are all great questions. They can be answered in a few simple words: I was desperate, she was calculated. Not desperate in a fall-on-the-floor-grabbing-ankles kind of way, just in a my-heart-wants-our-old-life-back kind of way. And I missed Lovie. She had been at the apartment; he had been absent. He was the one I missed at this point.

So how exactly did they end up moving into my apartment? They had been staying with his grandma in Hollywood when they'd come to town for work. Relations got strained between Pandora and Grandma so when everything blew up, I offered for them to move in with me, trying to save the day.

I did it for selfish reasons; I wanted to be a family again and I wanted to be back with him the way it was before. I had an inkling she was building up to this, she knew I would offer, and she needed an out from living at Grandma's. This was not a full-time arrangement, though. They still had the farm and were only coming down to Fort Lauderdale for three to four days most weeks and then heading back. The days depended on when Lovie had clients and if Pandora was teaching classes. Some weeks it would be Sunday night through Friday morning, and others it was super short, Tuesday night through Thursday night. They had keys to the apartment to come and go whenever; I cleared out the guest bedroom closet and set up the guest bathroom to accommodate their things. I even bought decorations that she picked out, so she felt at home.

There was an additional benefit for me. I took comfort in knowing that my house was not sitting vacant while I was gone. I was more comfortable knowing that when I would come home to an empty space, someone had been coming in and out keeping an eye on things. It made me feel more secure, especially with the Orlando incident just a couple of years before.

Old habits are hard to break. We planned dinners at home, then watched TV before heading to the only bed in the house.

They would invite me up to the farm occasionally for weekend visits. We attended art festivals, the mango festival, and local events. We had sexy time but not like we used to. There was always an underlying tension, everything seemed a little awkward. No one really knew how to interact in this new dynamic. I was constantly wondering if everything was okay.

The one thing we never did was cuddle. Fun and playtime were acceptable but nothing that showed any intimacy. Kissing was the hardest to navigate. One time it was allowed, another time it would break the mood and cause a "discussion."

Pandora's and my strained relationship became more evident. During this time, both of us were struggling with our feelings for each other. There had been so much hurt and resentment that the love was gone; neither of us was having any luck in getting it back. It was hard for me to reconcile if I even wanted to be with her. That meant I would need her approval and love, while at the same time working to heal myself. I was on eggshells constantly, but things were moving back in the direction I thought I wanted. The juice seemed worth the squeeze. There is no doubt in my mind we were both trying to make it work because of Lovie.

She knew he wanted to play with me. If she made me off-limits, he would find some way to have me. In order to stay one step ahead, she kept me around to make him happy at any given moment. I wanted to be his girlfriend, but knew he had chosen her, which meant I would have to make it work with her as well. If I wanted him, I had to have her. This statement has taken years to say out loud. It's hard to admit you've done things less than admirable in the quest for love but admitting it is necessary to grow and do better. I'll never say I was perfect or didn't make mistakes. I know I caused hurt. What I stand by is that I never had malicious intent. I never did anything with the thought of doing it just to "get back," trying to show "how it feels," or for the intention of causing emotional pain.

It was no shock to anyone this arrangement didn't last.

The catalyst that started to end it all happened one afternoon while she was getting ready in "her bathroom". She said something that made me feel as if she was trying to take over MY house. I actually talked back. This might be one of the first and only times that ever happened and she did not handle it well. I cannot recall exactly what the disagreement was about, but I will never forget that I felt strong standing up for myself. She was in my home. I was giving her a sanctuary from being at Grandma's house and I was not going to allow her to speak to me in a condescending tone. She was a guest, not a resident, in my house, and no, you can no longer speak to me as if I am your submissive. Period.

After that episode, they stayed less and less. It all came crashing down one morning when she left early for work. Lovie and I were still in bed, he was feeling frisky, and so we played. Because there's no point in lying, he told her what had happened, and she freaked out. Not just mad but actually had a full-on manic episode where she cussed him out, cussed me out, and then promptly removed every item they had at my place, declaring that this was the biggest betrayal of her life. To her, it must have been.

She couldn't grasp that she was not the be-all-end-all of my life anymore, and it must have been a major blow to her ego. She was excluded, had lost control of our situation, and couldn't handle that. I was a pawn for her. I was a test of his commitment and he failed.

Did I know it was "not allowed" for us to play? Yes. It's possible I subconsciously was trying to blow up the ship. But my bag of fucks was empty by then.

I spent three more months after they vacated in my quaint little apartment, in peace. This departure was another heartache, but not intense. I now understood that Pandora's love for me was gone as was mine for her. We wanted different things out of the relationship and were never going to be on the same page. That fact made me sad; we could have had it all. We could have conquered the world. However, I had a calm grasp on how negative we'd become for each other and knew it was time to let go, once and for all.

When my lease came up for renewal, I decided it was time for yet another change. Lovie's mom, Mama V, had a room available to rent for $700 and it just made sense for me to move in with her. We had always gotten along. She was always home, so my things would not sit in a vacant house, and she needed the additional income. She was the only family I had in South Florida and her rental rate was half of that anywhere else. It made sense.

Moving day was easy. Lovie helped me, and Pandora called him every thirty minutes to make sure that nothing was happening. I laughed because even if I had put out bait, he wasn't going to bite. He knew what was at stake and wouldn't risk his relationship with her. I was old news.

Once I was settled in at Mama V's, life moved on once again.

CHAPTER 9

NOT MY BEST LIGHTING

*"All human souls are connected which explains
why it hurts so much to detach from others"*
— Unknown —

I chose to name this chapter as I did because it includes the fifteen months in my life in which I made unflattering choices. It was a low point in decision making, it was a barrage of weight gain and loss. Several of the later months were drowned out by nightly drunkenness, and my choices were largely based around someone else.

Mama V was just what I needed during this time in my life. She was Aunt V at that time since no one was allowed to have roommates in the condo association where she lived, only family, so she called me her niece. It fit perfectly, she was half mother and half best friend, just like an aunt. She helped guide me as I got my shit together at that condo, which may sound strange after the above confession. She encouraged me to try new things, didn't judge me when I made mistakes and was an excellent sounding board for my emotional trauma. During the first several months I lived with her, there was very little communication between Pandora, Lovie, and me. And by very little, I mean none. They were doing their own thing.

Well, almost none. None except for occasional messages Lovie and I would send to each other through a chess app. We had been playing for a couple of years and just never stopped after the split. He's an excellent chess player and had simultaneous games going, so there weren't any red flags. It was innocent enough except for the ability to secretly communicate. I was the main one starting conversations, but he engaged. It would start simply and occasionally end with sexual innuendos.

Given this was the only lifeline I had to him, I would wait days or even weeks in between communication. Just knowing he was on the other end meant he was thinking of me. I knew he wasn't allowed to talk to me, but still laid out bait when I missed him. The idea that he chose her over me was too hard to grasp. I was the nice one. I was the one who would actually give him the life he wanted. My ego could not accept the finality of the situation.

One day I finally received a message through the chess app that made my heart stop. It started with "This is Mama." She had found our secret way of communicating and laid it out that he had agreed to never see or speak with me again- ever. It read like a mother telling the bad-influence friend that her kid would never be able to play again. Another disappointment, one of my own doing, which made it worse. What was my end game here? He wasn't coming back, why did I continue to torture myself?

Mama V and I talked about all this in depth. She bantered back and forth with me trying to understand the decisions he was making and dissect where I went wrong. She was Team Sarah all the way. She and Pandora got along fine in person but there wasn't a real connection. Neither of them actively tried to bond with the other. They had issues but I won't go into them because it's not my story to tell.

All of us are spiritual but not religious. We believe in a higher power, believe in the metaphysical, and believe that humans can have extraordinary abilities, such as psychics. We aren't talking about the cheesy carnival types, although I'm sure some of them do have special abilities. We are talking about psychics with a long history of being able to tap into energy sources.

I personally have only been to a psychic once, in 2016, and she did a reading based more on numerology. She asked very generic questions, got things like birthdate, times, etc., and then provided a synopsis of my past, present, and future track. Nothing uber specific but specific enough to make me reflect on choices and the future.

Mama V went to see a renowned physic while we were living together in 2015, for guidance on her career path and to get questions answered about her three boys. She was particularly interested in her oldest boy, Lovie. Was he on the right path? She took two photographs with her, one of me and one of Pandora. I'm not sure how she knew to bring those but she's tapped into her own energies, so....

When she got home, Mama V recounted what the psychic told her about all her questions and then brought out a recording from her session. When she was asked for images to help answer questions about Lovie, the psychic told her one has light energy that will be good for him and the other one has a dark energy. While there were no specifics on who was which energy, I assumed I was the light. After the psychic's prediction, I started to think there may have been problems in paradise.

Within a few weeks, Lovie began coming over to his mom's house, without Pandora, to spend time. Since I'd moved in, he stayed somewhat distant from Mama V so I know this shift in events made her heart happy. They would do mundane things like going out to eat and running errands together. I started being invited (secretly) to meet them when they were close to the condo. It was awkward at first. I struggled knowing I was in a gray area of cheating. I was off-limits, so even if we were in a public place, with his mother, Pandora had been very clear that he and I were to have no contact. He knew that. I also had her last message to me in that chat floating in the back of my mind, and I still participated. But, I mean, she wasn't *my* girlfriend anymore.

That gray area turned black and white quick. He'd had a key to Mama V's condo since she moved in just in case he ever needed it. One random morning I was startled awake when my bedroom door opened at six o'clock. There he was, casually walking into my bedroom like I should've been expecting him. Without a word, he closed the door behind him, climbed into bed and held me. I had not invited him. I did not know that he was coming. In fact, even in my wildest thoughts, I would not have imagined him climbing into bed with me.

This pattern continued for the next several weeks. I laid out an open invitation for him to come over as often as possible and Mama V was not upset when she saw him unexpectedly in the kitchen one morning. Surprised yes, but now she got to see her baby more often.

He got away with it because he lied to Pandora, saying he had a client in Weston. He would come over to sleep with me for an hour-ish, two to three times a week, then go back to his regularly scheduled program. We made love, talked about the issues they were having, and basked in the ability to hold each other. We talked about our future, how he was thinking he made the wrong choice. Plans were put together about how he was going to leave her.

All of this had unfortunate timing by the time it was all said and done though. During those weeks and months of no contact, I decided I was ready to leave my company of eight and a half years and try something different. A job had been offered to me that came with a considerable amount more money, based in Atlanta, and I would get the opportunity to help build a training department from the ground up. I was not unhappy in South Florida. I was not unhappy at Mama V's, but I was unhappy with myself and my life. A new career challenge was exactly what I needed, the chance to prove I was a leader. There was also a strong feeling, a pull, that I needed to go back to Atlanta, although I couldn't explain why.

Once my new contract was signed, I put in notice with my job and made arrangements to move to Atlanta. Lovie came over one morning with huge news: He was going to leave her and we would be together again officially.

Is this real life?? The thing I had been dreaming about for almost a year was finally happening. Only one downside, I was committed to moving back to Georgia. In-depth conversations followed on how we would make this work. I'd be traveling to South Florida monthly and could find ways to spend additional time. He would travel up if there was ever a long span of time before I could schedule another work trip. It was set. He left to spend the weekend at the farm with Pandora and lay all the cards on the table. That was one of the longest weekends of my life.

It was ninety-six hours of waiting. I knew it was a horrible idea to call or text him, it would make things worse. I didn't want to either. That's a lie. I did want to hear from him, but I wanted to respect the time he'd asked for. I was *not* going to make things harder. Besides, this was a totally fair request, especially given our history. Pandora was not going to take it quietly. She wouldn't say, "Okay cool, I get it." There would be fights and arguments. I convinced myself their breakup didn't involve me because he wasn't leaving her for me. He was leaving her because of their different opinions on what a polyamorous lifestyle meant. He was leaving her because she did not hold up her end of their bargain. He was leaving her because he was unhappy.

He assured me that he'd call with all the details the minute things were settled. Friday night I calmly read and watched shows with Mama V. I filled Saturday morning with as much "busy work" as I could find. My mind was busy creating scenarios of what was happening one hundred miles away, like a bad movie reel that was stuck on repeat. Saturday night I was a jittery mess and I started chain-smoking Sunday when there was still radio silence

I knew he had clients in Hollywood on Sunday night so, like a crazy stalker, I "had errands to run" and drove by the gym he worked at. My heart and stomach were in knots, and I made myself nauseous trying to guess what was happening. It had been three days of deafening silence while I waited for the green light on my future,

His car was not in the parking lot. Even if it had been, what was I gonna do? I could hear my heart pounding between my ears as my girl brain processed how crazy I was for driving twenty minutes to look for a parked car. As fate would have it, heading back home, I got stopped at an intersection. I randomly glanced to the right. A red Toyota Prius on the opposite side of the road was the first car in line waiting for the red light. I recognized the scene immediately. She was in the front seat, next to him.

It was another twenty-four hours before he called me. I was in complete agony now because of what I saw. So many scenarios played out in my head:

"Did he talk to her yet? Does she think everything is normal? Am I going to have to wait longer?"

"Of course, he talked to her. They are being shockingly civil. She must have had business in town. That's why she's with him. It's probably super uncomfortable being together."

"What if he chickened out and decided he doesn't want to deal with her drama right now? Are we going to have to hide longer? That would be the worst."

"Oh, God ... what if she was with him because she convinced him to stay together? No way. He was too adamant about leaving her. He must be so annoyed that he can't call me yet."

The worst was that Lovie and I would have to hide because he didn't talk to her.

This remains the actual worst conversation of my life. When he finally called me, the conversation was mostly him talking and me asking questions. As soon as I heard his voice, the very moment I answered the phone, I knew this was not going to end well for us. His voice was cold, exhausted, and emotionless. I walked outside the condo, down to my car, and started smoking again.

They were going to work it out. He gave me examples of why she was better than me and how she was more disciplined. He repeated stories back from her that were completely false. She lied to make herself look better. Life lesson here: Always speak your truth immediately, don't hold it inside. I never told him about the hurtful and mean conversations between me and her, and it came back to bite me in the ass, big-time. I couldn't defend myself, telling him those were lies only made me look desperate and would turn into a "she said" battle. When I brought up the "don't come home more than every two weeks" conversation, he flatly replied that she said that never happened. I was flabbergasted. It was evident then that anything I said was useless. Tears of anger, frustration, and pain gushed uncontrollably. It wasn't sadness in those moments, that came later, it was somewhere between shock and rage.

"I can't believe we have spent weeks planning a life together and now you're just telling me you changed your mind? This doesn't make any sense, like, I can't wrap my head around it. You tell me four days ago how miserable you are with her and now she's practically perfect compared to me? Answer me this: Do you love me?"

"I do love you, but I love her more."

He said, "I love her more." That was it for me.

I moved to Georgia in October of 2015, and we did not speak or communicate for four months. Not a peep.

A dear friend, Fran, opened her home and allowed me to join her family while I got back on my feet. She was part of the original bestie crew, back before I moved to Florida, who was married, had two amazing kids, and never missed an opportunity to speak her mind. She was nothing if not opinionated. She had a fiery spirit that allowed her to stand by her convictions, regardless of the consequences. If a store clerk said something she did not like, she would vow to never shop there again, and she never set foot in there again. This fire is also why she and I are no longer friends.

The devastation of Lovie's words repeated in my brain for months. I was literally—not figuratively, but literally—drunk in mismatched pajamas for three months. Just trying to make the words stop replaying by drowning them with liquor.

My new company had an office in north Atlanta near the trendy part of Sandy Springs. The amount of travel required was minuscule in comparison to my previous position, so each week I wasn't jet setting, they requested me in the office. This meant waking up by alarm clock, taking an early shower, and drudging through a morning commute. The plus side, I treated myself to several shopping sprees for new business attire. I'd been able to recycle outfits before, I saw new people each week. Now I saw the same people week after week. It was justified.

Each night after dinner, Fran would sit in the "mom" recliner, the kids sat on the sofa that was between us, and I propped myself up on the loveseat on the other side of the living room. We enjoyed movies or kids' shows on the massive TV until it was bath and bedtime for the littles. When she would come back down, we both would make another drink and turn on trash TV: *Real Housewives of (Every City)* or *Below Deck*. She listened to my incessant whining about him, my poor life choices, and how lost I was. Her constant response: reminding me of all the horrible things that he'd done over the last six years. Her goal was to make me realize I deserved better, that I was choosing to be sad and miserable. He certainly wasn't moping around, why should I. I went to bed crying most nights. I thought my life was over, my soulmate was gone, and I would never meet anyone who wanted me again. It was ugly.

I don't know how she put up with me for so long. She pushed me to get back in the dating scene, even if just to save her own sanity.

Who am I kidding? I was never *in* the dating scene. Fran urged me into it. I joined Plenty of Fish (pof.com), farmersonly.com, and tinder.com which resulted in two whole dates with two different men. Both men were lovely, dating was awful.

Engaging in random conversations daily with different strangers, knowing it was going nowhere 99.8 percent of the time, was mentally exhausting. And dumb. I don't care about the hiking you pretend to do, and I absolutely don't want unsolicited dick pics. Ewww. Is this really all that's out there? Has society produced this caliber of people? I decided to pass on that activity until I was a little more ready.

Remember I mentioned earlier I felt a pull back to Georgia that I couldn't explain? The real reason was shortly revealed to me in a horrific way January of 2016. I was sitting in an airport bar in Dallas, Texas, waiting on a flight home when I answered a phone call from my absolute best friend. Everyone around me became a blur, the background noise disappeared, as JR described what the doctors had found.

What the doctors found? I was swirling in confusion.

Seemingly out of nowhere, her husband had been diagnosed with melanoma, again, and this time it had spread to his brain and possibly his lungs. It was advanced. He was refusing chemo. It didn't look good. I couldn't believe what she was saying. Yes, he'd been losing weight three months ago at Halloween, but he'd been trying to lean out. Yes, New Year's Eve he looked ridiculously skinny, but he'd had a flu thing, so it made sense. Now she was telling me it'd been cancer the entire time.

The next several weeks were filled with doctor visits and updated prognoses on how long he had to live. Their daughter, my sweet niece, was not even a year old yet. I spent as much time as possible to help any way I could. Bring over dinners, groceries, wine, diapers, razors ... anything she needed.

Lovie and her husband, Cory, had always gotten along great. Over the years we would stay at their house when visiting from Florida and there where days we only saw the boys for dinner. They'd be out shooting or hiking or doing whatever it was they did. When the prognosis came back that he only had a couple of months to live and his motor functions were starting to weaken, I felt the right thing to do was to call Lovie so he could choose to say goodbye.

I dreaded making that call. It had been four months and I didn't know if he would even answer my call, but my gut told me the right thing to do was to reach out. We talked for one hour and four minutes. One hour was just about Cory, the other four minutes were about the dogs and animals on the farm. Nothing else was mentioned. I told Lovie if he wanted to call or text Cory, he needed to do so soon because time was running out. After we hung up, I did not communicate with him for another two months. I tried to call once or twice to give updates, but he never answered. I assumed that was the last time I would speak to Lovie.

Since 2005, JR and I have taken a girls trip. We've only missed two years; one the year she had her sweet baby and the year I moved to Florida. Given how much stress she was under, caring for her sick husband in hospice at their home, working full time, and mothering a one-year-old, she needed a break. But instead of taking our usual road trip, we decided the Blue Ridge Mountains, only about an hour and a half away, was the best choice. She deserved a break, and this was the perfect place for her to recharge. We drank bottles of wine, lived on cheese and crackers, scrapbooked, and watched Disney movies all weekend.

When my phone rang one early afternoon during a scrapbook session, I was shocked to see what name popped up. It was Lovie. It had been eight weeks since we had the Cory conversation and six months since we'd talked about anything else. I stepped outside on the front porch to smoke, not wanting to tell JR who it was yet. I couldn't even be sure it was him on the other end. Maybe Pandora had seen my name in the call log, thought we were communicating, and wanted to confront me. I was finally in a better place, now that I had something actually worth giving attention to and I didn't have the capacity (or desire) to hear her voice. I sat down on the top stair, lit up, and warily answered.

"Hello?" My best attempt to be pleasant-ish but not available. It was either that or "WHAT?"

"Hey!" He always sounds so cheery.

"Hey ..." I softened my greeting because I heard his voice, but was still unsure of why he was calling. This could be a trap.

"What are you up to right now?"

"JR and I are on our girl's trip right now. Someone she works with has a cabin they let us use for the weekend up in Ellijay. It's beautiful."

"Cool! Is Cory with y'all?"

"No. He's not able to get up anymore. His parents came to stay with him for the weekend so she could have a break."

He continued asking all the things, "How are you? How've you been? What've you been up to?" "How's JR?" "Anything new with Cory?"

After a few minutes of pleasantries, he turned the conversation to how he was unhappy and opened up about what was going on with Pandora. I didn't ask a single question; he was on a roll. The way he was talking shocked me because it was so uncharacteristic of him to just blurt out negativity or open up about personal issues. I kept thinking, "What is happening and why is he calling me now?"

The way he expressed frustration about her gave me a feeling of satisfaction. I wasn't proud of it but I felt smug listening to him vent. Both of them had patronized me, and now the tables were turning. At the end of the day though, the heart always wins out over the brain. This was the conversation that brought us back to life.

I had other focuses now; he was not my main concern. I didn't want to spend too much time on this call, but I needed every juicy detail. I'm a terrible human for this but hearing him say all the negative things about her that she'd said about me, was validating. I was not, in fact, the problem. I wrapped up my end of the conversation by telling him Fran and I had a cruise booked the end of March out of Fort Lauderdale so there might be a possibility he and I could meet then but, for now, I needed to head back inside.

"I think I can make that happen."

After hearing words I assumed were an empty promise, I hung up and went inside.

I did nothing logistically to facilitate the meet up. I simply gave him the specifics, when he asked, on where I would be and when. The ball was completely in his court. If there was a desire to see me, he would have to make all the effort. There was a brief window of time between getting back into port and when our flight left to go back home to Georgia.

And by brief window, I mean like four hours. That's not a lot of time to disembark from a cruise ship and wait for the painful inefficiency of the Fort Lauderdale Airport's TSA team to clear you through security. Luckily, I am a master of logistics. Truly, I can work schedules and times better than most. If I forfeited the pre-flight bar drink, there were twenty-five minutes of available time. Obviously, that is not enough to do more than say hi and bye, so I figured he would bail.

Nope. He drove an hour round trip to the airport parking garage, sat and waited until I walked out. Not the classiest, but what's more romantic than an airport reunion?

Fran was not happy about this meeting. I'd been on her sofa, drunk and crying for months. She waited inside the airport while I walked to the parking lot; her displeasure at the situation was scathing. I can't blame her, who would condone that shit show starting again?

It was shortly after this trip that Fran and I started to drift apart. Not because I pulled away and put my attention just on him, I actually didn't do that completely this time. I had a new defense system up so he couldn't get back in too quickly. Ok, not a strong system but let's call progress, progress. We drifted apart because Fran disagreed with my speaking to Lovie again. She definitely was against us getting back together and didn't think it was the right (or sane) thing to do. Being a woman with deeply held opinions and principles, she cut me out because she couldn't get behind my choice. Because she had spent so much time picking me off the floor, she'd stopped seeing me as a friend and saw me as a helpless adolescent she needed to mother. Within a year of our cruise, we were no longer communicating. The loss was sad for me, especially as our relationship deteriorated and the awkwardness became more palpable. The more I feel judged, the faster I shut down.

That day in the Fort Lauderdale airport garage, it had been over seven months since I'd felt Lovie's lips on mine. Sitting in the passenger seat of that old Honda Odyssey was surreal. He had made the effort to come to me and I had some of my power back. We kissed and held each other in long embraces with no words. We spent fifteen minutes together, but he promised to come up to Georgia, just like before, to see me. He and Pandora were done. They were officially broken up and there was no way I could be blamed for it. I'd been out of the picture for over six months and their issues were all on them. This was the first time since Orlando, four years earlier, that we would be together, without lies, deception, or limits. I promised myself to never do that again.

He kept his word and came up to visit in April. I was still living in Fran's house with two young kids, it wasn't appropriate to ask if he could stay there. It would have also been incredibly rude and insensitive to ask her to allow him into her home, even with no kids, given how unhappy she was about this reunion. I booked a hotel room for a couple of nights.

A couple of nights turned into a week. Then Cory took a quick downward turn. Lovie extended his stay to be there for me. We went over to spend time at JR and Cory's house; I spent a couple of nights there while he stayed in the hotel. On April 21, 2016, Cory passed. I got the call during a training class from which I had to excuse myself in order to process the news. Once again, Lovie extended his stay.

He picked me up at work, drove us back to our hotel so I could cry and get my emotions in check for JR. I packed a bag and he drove me to be with her. I was so happy to have someone as my rock as I was that day. It was not about me or my feelings. My best friend in the whole world just lost her partner after years of marriage and months of agony. I needed someone to be there for me, so I could be there for her. All in, his long weekend trip to Georgia was now over two and a half weeks.

Trips between South Florida and Georgia started happening monthly but there was something missing. The vibe, the passion, the excitement all wore off quickly. Phone calls and texts stopped being flirty. They were just ... boring. I was at the high end of my recent weight and my physique was a constant point of contention for him. He wanted freedom. He'd been in a relationship for the better part of the last decade and needed to spread his wings. My weight gave him something to use as a catalyst.

Lovie and Pandora were still living together, having sex but nothing more than friends with benefits. He told me they had separate bedrooms, and living together was simply a matter of convenience. Neither of them wanted to move out or to sell the property so they had to make it work. Are you wondering why the house was an issue at this point since I bought it solely in my name three years earlier? Why was I not able to just list it and move on? Great question.

Between the time I moved out in fall 2013 and when they "moved in" part-time with me during spring of 2014, Lovie and Pandora sold the parcel of raw land they'd purchased to build the shipping container home on. The profits made from that sale were enough to pay off the remaining mortgage loan. Physical title in hand, I made good on my original promise to sign it over to them. So many people have said I shouldn't have signed it over or asked why I did such a stupid thing. Hell, I ask myself why I did. Was I really that weak? The only response I can give is "I said I would." Regardless that our relationship was over, I committed to signing it over. I don't regret it. It took strength, not weakness, to follow through on that. It boils my blood to think about it, but a deal is a deal.

I was honest in those first few months Lovie and I were back together about where I stood with him dating both Pandora and me: I couldn't handle it. I was uncomfortable with their living arrangement. The scars of the last year were still too fresh. I no longer pretended that I was okay with it. She and I were months beyond our last conversation ever spoken and there was no more sharing. I never gave an ultimatum; there was not one to give. He didn't have to choose between us, but I couldn't compete anymore for his attention. I was eight months into healing and at peace, knowing he might walk away without another glance back. At peace does not mean that I would have been okay with it, but I wouldn't crumble to pieces. That would be his choice.

There is a fine line between ultimatums and boundaries, but individual experiences tend to help define where that line is. I believe it's the intent and delivery that separate them. Every action has a reaction. We are all imperfect, we all need work, so compromise and commitment must be considered. During research for this book, I spoke to several women whom I greatly respect to get their take on the nuances of the concepts. It took processing from everyone polled to get a semi-solid "final answer." The depth that is required to dive into ultimatums versus boundaries accurately and fairly is far beyond the scope of my story or academic level. Many brilliant minds have extensive research on this topic; it's worth the time to check them out. Since this is my story, I have my brief and surface-level breakdown of where I see the line, at this point in my life.

Ultimatums are final deal breakers that have a defined consequence and are externally focused. They are about threatening, about trying to control someone else and typically happen after an issue has already come up. Ultimatums might be seen as necessary for serious offenses but need to have a timeline and defined course for correction. The core intention of an ultimatum, you are trying to change the other person.

Boundaries can be more fluid, and consequences are often left undefined or unspoken. They are internally focused based on your level of self-awareness. A boundary has an intent of positive guidelines of expectations to protect your own authentic self and they are ongoing conversations. Here, you might be requesting a change anyone's behavior or actions, but the liability of making a final decision of action falls on you.

My boundary was no Pandora. Lovie's line was no fluffy chicks. My weight had not changed much, and he was losing physical attraction to me. He wanted a girlfriend fitting his ideal standards: tall, dark, lean, big ass. He wanted more than me. That part was fine, we had been talking about finding a girlfriend for us. The issue was I lacked the discipline to lose weight. I talked about it but never executed any real plan to follow through. His delivery on this subject was harsh but honest.

It began to click for me: Fitness and eating right isn't about weight loss, it's about loving yourself and being healthy. Weight loss is the bonus. I hadn't done anything just because I loved myself, I'd been doing everything to make someone else love me. I was miserable in my skin but lacked the self-love to do anything about it. That's a hard pill to swallow.

By late July, he started dating someone new. I found out from a YouTube notification. The only videos he posted were beehive updates but watching them made me feel connected to him somehow. This video was a walk-through of the farmhouse. Pandora asked him to take a video when he got to the house to prove her bedroom door was locked and document what the house looked like. In the last few seconds, there was a brief clip with a woman's poofy hair showing in the corner. He was not alone. Ugh- crushed again. It just was not our time.

This new woman was young, gorgeous, voluptuous, and a mom. The kid part both threw me and scared me. At twenty-five, Lovie had a vasectomy to ensure that he would never have children of his own. He had a loose policy of not getting serious with anyone with kids. Seeing him date someone and not minding that major piece of her life made me think he was madly in love with her. Maybe this was his perfect woman, and he was willing to give up all his old ways just to be with her. Maybe this really was the actual end of our relationship. My insecurities were raging. Sidenote: I love the children that are in my world and I would do anything, absolutely anything, for my littles. However, when I got divorced at twenty-six, my desire to have children just went away. I saw what all my friends were going through as single parents, or even married but there was still one primary caregiver, and I decided I liked my freedom too much. Having someone completely dependent on me was more than I wanted to sign up for. I feel like the universe had other plans for me as well because I have never been pregnant, not even a pregnancy scare.

Our communication was sparse during this summer timeframe, he was preoccupied. Nothing more than a text message here or there. I put my girl brain to good use with the help of my Boo. Boo and Lovie grew up together and are best friends to this day, twenty-eight years later. They dated in high school but life took them in different directions. I meet her through Lovie back in 2009 when he was still living in Georgia. Boo had made a couple life changes and ended up moving back to Georgia around the same time I did in 2015. I reached out to try and make a connection. She definitely made me work for our friendship but it was worth it.

Since the time when Lovie and I reconnected, Boo and I had gotten pretty close. She could ask all the questions and get all the scoop without sounding suspicious because her and Lovie were besties. She never told me anything about their conversations. She did not have to. I was usually there, in the kitchen "cooking," listening to their calls on speaker. Not my finest moments but inquiring minds wanted to know, and I wasn't going to ask her directly. I hoped the relationship with Lovie's new girlfriend was temporary. We didn't break up, there was no split, we just fizzled way down. I needed to know just how serious this new flame was. I would be in South Florida working so I invited him to come see me in my hotel. He agreed. We hashed out the dates, times, and I told him to pack a bag. That meant "plan to stay the night" and his agreeing meant we were having a slumber party.

The day of our rendezvous I was having drinks with a dear friend beforehand. I texted him to confirm his ETA and something in my mind said I needed to ask about his sleepover bag. His response: "I'm not staying the night." I promptly called him to get clarification on why he changed the plans we'd had set for weeks.

"What do you mean you're not staying the night?"

"The girl I'm seeing doesn't want me to sleep with anyone else."

"And? I'm not some random chick."

"I never said I was spending the night." To him, agreeing just meant hanging out, there was no need to elaborate on the fact that he had no intention of staying the night.

"Why did you think I was telling you to pack a bag?" I'd started to lose my cool. He knew what I meant by that. He just avoided addressing it to save himself the headache of explaining.

"Do you not want me to come over then?"

Fighting back tears of frustration, I told him to still come over and rushed off the phone.

Are you fucking kidding me? He has always been up front and open about not being monogamous and never getting married again. Was he actually that serious with her? She asked for monogamy and he said okay? Everything about these facts seemed to signal this was a temporary scenario, yet his actions indicated otherwise. He was willing to do monogamy?

I got back to the hotel, trying to get my thoughts together, there was so much adrenaline coursing through my body. There were no tears. My friend had helped me turn insecurities into strengths. I was not going to be a side chick. I was going to be the one who chose the next path; I would not just sit back and follow along with whatever he gave me. He had to decide to be in or out. After almost eight years, I finally stood up for what I wanted.

It wasn't long before he knocked on the door; I was ready to fight. That lasted the three seconds it took me to unlock the door. Weakness kicked in. First thing I noticed when I opened the door was how beautiful he was. It had been several weeks since I'd seen him. I let myself melt into his hug. The next thing I noticed was the lack of an overnight bag. That prompted my liquid courage to came right back, and I was ready to talk.

I stepped back, blocking his ability to come in further. The first thing I spoke was "You really aren't going to stay the night?"

"No, I told you, she doesn't want me playing with anyone but her, and I am not ready to give that up."

I took another step back from him. Holding eye contact, my throat was so parched that I feared I'd lose my voice. My feet were glued to that section of tacky carpet to keep him from moving into the room.

"If you're not going to stay, then you should leave. I have no desire to be friends and hang out platonically." I was using my formal business voice. And I meant it. Deep down I knew that I really meant those words. I loved him too much to hang out and pretend to be just friends.

The shock on his face was obvious. He probably heard my heart pounding rapidly in my chest; I was a buzzed, sweaty, nervous mess. He must have assumed I'd calm down and cave when I saw him, not that I'd draw a line in the sand. Never in thirty-three years had I stood firmly in face of a confrontation. Certainly, never to him, he'd only seen me cower or walk away during our years with Pandora.

We talked (okay fine, mainly I talked); some of it got heated. I explained why I was not budging this time, and he listened. I don't know what was actually going on in his head but I imagined it was something like, "Oh shit, she's serious. This might be the actual time she walks away." I hit my limit. I wanted a commitment from him and, more importantly, I knew I deserved better. Being a side chick would never again be a thing. I didn't give a fuck. The bag was empty for the second time. After so many years of back and forth, my heart still believed that he was my soulmate. I had grown enough to know sometimes you have to let go, be less available, stand up for yourself. Humans will push the limits of what they get away with unless you set boundaries. And I was clear with my boundaries that night. I kept repeating that same phrase every time he spoke, "I don't want to be friends." (Thank you, JB, for giving me the courage that night to stand up for what I wanted. You changed the course of my life forever. I love you).

Something I said had clicked for him. He stayed. He kissed me, we went to dinner, we played all night, and then we went to breakfast before I had to go to work. I was not around for the conversation he had with the new girlfriend but I know he told her everything that happened and they did continue to see each other for a couple of months. I was never involved in that relationship, but we knew about each other, and he was up front with her when he was with me. She did not like that we were back together, but she chose to continue seeing him. In my head, I was his main relationship and since I was not involved with her, that made her the secondary. It was also difficult to put a lot of thought into their dynamic, it was temporary. She wanted monogamy; that was not an option on the table, so by default things would eventually just fizzle out. Had she been interested in poly, the story would have turned out very differently.

We have not slowed down since that night. There is definitely more to the story, but something kismet happened in that hotel room. I don't know how to explain it, but I can pinpoint this exact moment I knew our life together was ramping up.

The second pivotal moment happened just a couple of weeks later. He'd come up to see me in Georgia and we were not ready to part ways when he had to leave. Luckily, I had to travel to Orlando the following week, so we decided I would drive to meet him in Fort Lauderdale after work. It is only a two-and-a-half-hour drive, which is nothing compared to how many hours I had spent in the car over the years for work. There was something to look forward to, and then we had the greatest hotel party ever, and for the first time, it was just me and him.

This was the first time I recall him directly saying that he loved me. We were wrapped up together and he apologized, genuinely apologized, for everything: the things he said, the things he did, the decisions he had made. He was honest about a lot of things and for the first time, possibly ever, spoke to me from his heart.

I thought seriously about marriage for the first time that night. Of course, that's always been my relationship goal, but it never seemed feasible. At a random point in the evening, while we were standing in the bathroom, he just looked at me and said, "Blah blah something, Sarah Jolicoeur." I couldn't get those words out of my head. An entirely new level had been reached and gave me the first glimmer that marriage might be on the table. I might actually end up marrying this man.

CHAPTER 10

THE SAME FIGHT –
ONE LAST TIME

"Don't fight a battle if you don't gain anything by winning"
— Erwin Rommel —

It had been a rocky year for us up to this point. To recap, Lovie and I spoke for the first time again in March, saw each other in April, peaked and fizzled from July until October when he started dating someone new, and then we had those two magic hotel parties that sent us back into paradise. Pandora was still in the picture at this point, and although they were completely broken up, there was still joint custody of the house, as well as a friendship. Bitter moment here, how or why they were still friends at this point is beyond me. I hated that they were still having sex, but I understood why. It was an arrangement of conveniences. He assured me over and over it was just sex. He didn't want to start any relationships without me, so it was sex with her or nothing.

He moved out of the master into the guest bedroom, but I was skeptical of how often he shared her bed all night. I would FaceTime him to see his surroundings without point-blank asking what bed he was in. Nobody likes a woman who nags and parades her insecurity. I just tried to be subtle although, I am pretty positive he always knew what I was doing. Luckily for me, he went along without calling me out. We were sole-ly communicating via phone during that month, so it wasn't that suspicious. I was *forbidden* from being on the property. I wasn't going to go to the house anyway, but I did have a new-found confidence in his commitment to me so I chose to not harp on that point.

Over Thanksgiving, I went to visit my parents in the north-ern part of the US. A) Burrrrr 2) I would only travel north of the Mason-Dixon line for my parents; it is miserable there. I was so excited to tell them that Lovie and I were going to make another go at it and that this time really felt different. It was over that weekend that Lovie and I booked a four-night cruise for Christmas. OMG. This was happening. While I was Polly Positivity, Mom and Dad were a little more reserved in their excitement. Lovie had been to a couple of family events but never spent significant time around them. The majority of what they knew was from our past; not positive.

Lovie joined me at a work conference at Universal Studios Orlando just after that Thanksgiving holiday. Tuesday night, he arrived late, and we spent the night making love after weeks apart. Wednesday night started off the same way, comfortable conversation while I freshened up before dinner. Out of no-where, he dropped a bomb on me. This had become a predict-able pattern, yet still surprised me. I was putting makeup on in the bathroom, he casually mentioned from the living area that he and Pandora had been discussing possibly starting to date again. I stopped applying eyeliner and stared in the mir-ror blankly, wondering what he was going to say next. Surely, I'd heard wrong.

I heard correctly. Then this man had the nerve to ask me how I felt about that. How did I feel about that? Seriously? It took me a minute to fully process those words and recover from the knockout feeling I had in my chest. You'd think I'd be used to this conversation by now, nope. Shocked every time. There were no tears this time, just disbelief. I didn't feel mad or particularly sad. I felt tired.

I knew in my heart there couldn't be another rewind. I was not able to mentally or physically put myself through those scenarios when previous track records had me as the underdog. The idea of putting energy into planning a life we'd build together, just for him to switch teams again, was inconceivable. Thanks, but no thanks. A humiliating reel of those first few months apart flashed into my head as a warning. I could feel energy leaving my body as the seconds passed but the conversation had started, so needed to be finished. And there was more.

Pandora's pitch to him went something like this and obviously I'm not quoting: They would find a girlfriend together. She promised they would be best friends with all the benefits, and he could have his freedom too. It would be different than before. The only exception, he could not have me in any capacity as a relationship.

She is toxic to me, complete poison, as I am to her. There was no desire to be around anyone associated with her, including him. This is the woman who was manipulative and cunning toward me in every breath she took. This is the woman who still blamed me for them not working out. I take responsibility for my wrongdoings; I wish she would do the same. But she stands firm that she holds no responsibility. This is the woman who was verbally abusive, so I would comply as a submissive, obedient girlfriend. And now, sitting in the same hotel room him and I made love in for hours the night before, he brings this idea to the table as a discussion. He tells me all the things she's promised and what the cost would be.

I refused to give her any control over my life or who was in it. I had already set that boundary months ago, I was not willing to go down that road again. So, when he asked what I thought of it, I knew immediately it was a make-or-break conversation. Our exchange of words was brief and calm. I was firm about my opinion: He was free to do whatever he wanted, but I would not be a part of it. I was not open to revisiting a relationship arrangement she was involved in. He and I started a new party where she was not invited. He did approach this subject gently and as an open discussion. He understood where I was coming from, assured me he wouldn't agree to anything where I was out. He just wanted to feel out how I would react and with that we tabled it, hoping it was over.

Well, dinner was awkward. The issue was not tabled, in fact, it carried on throughout the entire night and got progressively more intense. No matter how hard I tried, I couldn't let it go. I tend to make horrible jokes or smile too much when trying to cover up emotions I don't think I should be having. Despite my desperate efforts, the nagging pit in my stomach never went away. It was like my body physically telling me she was never welcome to be in my world (willingly) again.

Just the right number of alcoholic drinks are always my allies and I needed them on the Uber ride home that night. The conversation heated back up because Pandora began texting him and I got pouty. Not only had the subject of her dominated my night, but I'd started getting more irate at him for even asking me about this arrangement after knowing how I felt. They can have any discussions they want, she can make any request of him, that's between them. But he is not required to bring those ideas to me, it's his prerogative to just leave bad ideas dead in the water. Why did he even mention it? The pinnacle of this fight happened when Lovie got angry–actually angry—at me for being a giant ball of big emotions. That poor Uber driver, he didn't know what was happening ... until the screaming match started.

"I am the one who gets shafted and chastised for crying and being upset but I'm not the one bringing the drama. EVER. I have never given ultimatums. I have never restricted you but when she gives these ultimatums and I don't *agree* to them, I am the bad guy. Go blow yourself, this is not on me."

Clearly–*clearly*–I was NOT intended to see the text messages she was sending during all this. Pandora had been texting him all night and when he wasn't responding, these came through. These are direct quotes because I took a screenshot of them from his phone and sent them to myself that night, in the back of the Uber. Judge me all you want.

10:22 pm: I love you.

10:25 pm: Be strong baby ... you got this

10:44 pm: She loves you .... whatever you give ... she will take. But she will try to seduce you ... that is what she does. Good luck ... because she is very good. She knows you. She knows your weakness. I comes (sic) to your will baby. I believe in you. No matter what.

10:45 pm: But I have no desire to fight Sarah. My white flag is raised. But I do want to try to make it work with you. I hope you want the same too.

I lost my fucking shit. The tears just fell down, not from sadness but from straight anger. "I love you?" That's not a statement made by someone you're *thinking* about dating. Then he started in on me again like I was the cause of this. Fuck that. We have established that I am a crier and this time was no different. I was ugly crying because I'd never experienced outrage like this.

I was hurt that he'd even ask. I was livid that her bullshit once again came back on me, and she somehow manipulated the scenario to make him see me as the problem. I was flabbergasted that somehow this fight was now my fault. It was difficult for me to get words together and express myself; I was not forming cohesive sentences. I did finally get enough words together to scream, "It's not fair she creates the drama and I'm the one who has to deal with the shit show," as I stormed out and slammed the Uber van door in his face. This night is in the top three worst verbal conversations that we've had ... ever.

It took time for both of us to process. The next day was strained. I was unsure if I could open my heart because he had actually brought this option to the table, after everything. He'd asked permission to violate my boundary. I was disappointed that we had argued, I cannot handle us being upset at each other for more than a few minutes, but I knew this was not on me. Spending the next day at Universal Studios park, standing in lines, just the two of us, was torture. I wanted to ask a million questions but not wanting to hear answers. I'm a fixer and wanted to make everything normal again. I wanted to ask if they had texted that morning. Did he tell her about our fight? Did he listen to me and take what I said to heart? Where was his head now? He was saying he wanted to be with me, but could I believe him? Something happened gradually, a shift in words that nullified the idea of them dating again to a gentle conversation about our future ... and what my Christmas present would be.

Lying in bed with his arm around me and my head on his chest, I nudged for hints on what he was getting me. Once I'd narrowed it down to jewelry, I started to get giddy. A ring. It had to be a ring. This was huge, especially after the epic level of anger two days ago. I guess this means he's sticking around.

December rolled on without any more conversation about Lovie and Pandora getting back together. He invited me to spend Christmas in South Florida with his family before we sailed out on the cruise we'd booked over Thanksgiving. We had been together for the better part of almost eight years, and an invite for Christmas with his family was another sign that he wanted to move forward. My girl brain hoped that he would propose. We had not had any conversations about marriage specifically but there was that time he called me Sarah Jolicoeur, followed by the comment he liked the ring of it, and then there was the teaser in Orlando about getting jewelry. This idea was solidified when he was texting with Boo about Christmas options for me ... and they were rings. Of course, she was supposed to keep it a secret, but we were in the car together when he texted her three different options to choose from. She may have shown me the text and I may have pointed at my favorite one. I knew it was happening.

Sitting in Mama V's living room Christmas Day, I tried to keep my cool. Just go with the flow. Don't make it obvious that I was expecting a big grand gesture. In my head, I had worked out hundreds of ways he would present me with this ring.

One element that was consistent in my fantasies, he would get down on one knee in front of me and said something romantic, but not too romantic because he's not into lovey-dovey stuff. He never has been. Seeing a person get on one knee is something I have dreamed about since being a little girl. The image of the person you love kneeling in front of you, a vulnerable position, with a symbol of their love and commitment to you, verbalizing devotion is the epitome of life goals. When my ex-wife and I got engaged, it was lame. We were sitting in a hair salon and one of us said something to the effect of "Should we get married?" To which the other replied, "Sounds good." We went and bought an engagement ring at Jared, promptly followed by a trip to Barnes and Noble to purchase wedding planning books. No frills, nothing special. Just an average daily decision, similar to ones we had about where to eat dinner. I loved it at the time, I still treasure that memory today, it is part of my story. But it was no Hallmark moment.

I avoided opening his gift until last in order to ensure maximum dramatic effect. There weren't massive amounts of gifts, but my family sent a gift to Mama V's house for me. My family truly is the best. I was seated on the loveseat; Lovie was next to me and casually handed me a box. Initially, I was a little confused because the box was not a ring-box shape, it was flat, the kind you might expect for a bracelet or necklace. Okay, he is trying to throw me off just in case Boo told me. As I opened it, he sat still next to me. No movement was made towards the floor. Okay, he wants me to fully open it, then he will get on one knee. As I got the wrapping paper carefully removed (again for dramatic effect) and started to open the box, I saw one of *my* rings in the box along with a folded piece of paper. Ummmm.

I started unfolding the paper, turning my head to my left, where he was still sitting on the couch, and gave him a cute but confused glance. Printed on the paper was a giant image of the ring I had pointed to on Boo's phone. It was gorgeous. One large sapphire stone in the middle with a tiny halo of diamonds surrounding it. The sides made a crisscross giving the appearance of an infinity sign. The picture looked beyond what I ever could have expected, even though it was just a piece of paper. However, he gave me no signs of what it meant.

He grinned, explaining that he had snuck a ring out of my jewelry bag so there would be something in the box but my real ring hadn't come in on time. His sweet face was so proud of this gift. I, on the other hand, had to compose myself because that was all he said. I was at the intersection of reality and storytelling and needed to fix my face—quick.

There was no proposal or explanation of what the ring meant. All that buildup was completely made up in my head. His gesture was endearing, and I didn't want to appear disappointed in his gift. I took the ring out of the box, placed it on my left hand, quieted my inner monologue, and made a big deal about it. This was the grandest gesture he'd made, and it meant everything, even if it wasn't a proposal. Progress was being made.

Day-after-Christmas shopping is almost as magical to me as the entire Christmas season. It's a tradition that I have held onto for my entire adult life. This particular year though, there was only one quick stop the day after and that was Charming Charlie to buy myself a placeholder ring. Tragically, Charming Charlie is no longer around, but it was a magical place filled with an obscene amount of costume jewelry, all organized by color. Anything you could think of from dresses to purses to rings was there. I didn't find an exact replica of the ring on paper, but I was not getting on our cruise ship without a new ring. Finding the closest thing I could, I slipped it on my finger and off we sailed.

Ever since my first cruise, I've been addicted. Complete disconnection from technology, miles of tranquil ocean farther than you can see, food available twenty-four hours a day, a crew willing to wait on you hand and foot, the ability to forget everything outside that floating paradise, there is nothing else like it. Of course, my favorite part of traveling with Lovie is the uninterrupted togetherness. On average we sail twice per year, always in an interior room. The Universe gave us an early wedding present this particular year, an interior room that overlooked the promenade. The promenade is where all the action is.

We were sitting in the bay window looking at everyone below exploring the ship. It seemed like a good moment to find the courage to ask about the symbolism of the ring. Both of us were giddy with cruise excitement, still high from Christmas cheer and intense infatuation from being apart. My question came from an open heart and mind.

It was a beautiful conversation because he didn't provide me with the answers I wanted, but gave me a truthful indication of where he saw our life together headed. This ring was more of a promise ring, he was committed to me, committed to building a life together from this point on. We agreed we wanted another partner sooner than later. He painted a picture of the vision he had for what a girlfriend would look like and how we would all interact. I did more agreeing than talking, optimistic that there was no new information coming to me. He reassured me since I made it past the two-year and the five-year and then the seven-year mark, he knew he didn't want to do life without me. That promise might mean marriage later on but for now, it was a symbol of his commitment to me.

CHAPTER 11

WEDDING BELLS

Marriage, then in love, that was how our path went. I was wildly in love with him and he had love for me. I don't know if he was in love with me at this point, you'd have to ask him, but I know he said he was certain that he didn't want to lose me again and wanted me in his life forever. I also know that he would do anything to make me happy—including getting married— which he said he would never do again.

A lot of people ask why we got married legally, especially when we are considered unconventional. I believe in the act of committing to the vows that you say, and they mean something. The rings you wear will be a reminder of those promises when things get hard, when you want to give up and walk away. I admit, I do also love shiny things, especially diamonds, so those are a bonus. There is also the name change; I'm traditional. I wanted a new last name legally. I love my family name, but I worked really hard for this new one. There are a lot of vowels at the end of his last name and it's hard to spell. Admittedly, I waited until it was mine before putting effort into it. I still spell it out loud more often than I care to admit.

The traditional vows "to have and to hold, in sickness and health, for better or worse" (or any other general version of those words) are an acknowledgment that it won't always be glitter and rainbows. One of us will get sick, have surgeries with long recovery times, or there will be times that we're just sick of each other. There will be fights but we made a promise to fight fair. We will get better together, we will grow together, and we will hold on to each other through all the amazingness that we experience. Our support system that is family and friends will always be surrounding lights, but now it's us at the core. We must always choose us first. The "until death do us part," I feel neutral about. I believe souls have different journeys on earth and through each reincarnation, we find each other again. As soul mates, we always have and always will be connected in each lifetime.

The spiritual concepts of soul mates and twin flames are fascinating to me. If you're into "woo woo" stuff, do a quick Google search and see if you're lucky enough to have both in your life. Lovie and I are soul mates. We are two separate souls, linked together by an extraordinary bond. Twin flames are when one soul splits into two bodies. Lovie has a twin flame: Boo. They are the truest, most spot-on definition if there ever was one, which explains why I love her too much. They think alike, act alike, say similar things, have similar dispositions, and even favor in looks. It's incredible. I, on the other hand, haven't come across my twin flame yet.

Being faithful and true are the most important promises in marriage. We are non-monogamous and yet the last six years we have been faithful to each other.

Do we sleep with other people: yes

Has he "hung out" with someone else during our early years of marriage: yes

Have I: yes

But we don't keep secrets. I express how I feel and he tells me where he stands. Our marriage continues to evolve and we make decisions together. The word faithful is a synonym for honesty and respect. Being true doesn't mean there is no hurt, it means there are no lies.

No further engagement talk happened on the cruise, but my ring did arrive the night we got back to Georgia for New Year's Eve. It was the perfect start to 2017.

Valentine's Day weekend, Boo, her sister Lissa, Lovie, and I went on The Tour d'Florida. It was a fitting name for a road trip we made up. We left Georgia with an outline of destinations but there was no actual plan. Just follow whatever whim hits us.

The first stop was two nights in Tampa to visit Lovie's brother and his wife. We continued south for a quick stop in at the farm so Lissa and Boo could see it. Pandora did not know we were there because I was not allowed to be on the property ... she had forbidden it. That's what she said. She *forbid* him to bring me onto the property. From there we crossed Alligator Alley to spend one night in a North Miami beachfront resort. My travel with Hilton hotels paid off when we walked into a two-bedroom, last minute for free on points, massive suite. Our last stop was one night in Orlando, at a hotel with a full water park on-site. The entire trip we laughed, drank, and ate until we passed out every night, exhausted from living each day to the max.

For all the fun this trip was, the most significant parts were in the conversations while driving. All in, we spent over twenty hours in the car, plenty of time for heavy discussions. It was during the first leg, from Georgia to Tampa, the idea of us getting married became a real discussion. One of the two "neutral" parties in the back seat brought it up. I can't remember if it was Boo or Lissa.

There were financial benefits as well as the emotional benefits to us uniting in marriage. I knew he wasn't ready to consider marriage for emotional reasons. His disinterest in labels or getting married again was no secret. But I knew that money talked to him in a different way. Team Marriage needed to present this from a rational, financial standpoint.

It might sound like I was minimizing myself or willing to settle for whatever he would give. In a way, that is true. I was not under the disillusionment getting married would suddenly change the state of our relationship. He lived full time in Florida, me in Georgia, and we were together once a month-ish. The words "I love you" were said rarely, if ever. He was still casually dating the same woman from last fall, but that had almost hit its expiration. I knew that getting married, having the husband-and-wife label, would only enhance our dynamic. I know how Lovie's brain works. I just needed to speak his language, so he'd get out of his own way.

He'd come to Georgia in February for Tour d'Florida, so it was my turn to travel down. On March 3, two weeks after Tour d'Florida, I got to South Florida and the "should we, shouldn't we get married" conversation picked right back up. It really wasn't a discussion, more like a pros and cons list. I should've gotten an award for my acting skills while trying to play it cool during this talk. Heading back home from Costco, something on the list clicked for him. He looked at me and said, "Okay, let's do it."

I was momentarily stunned. My inner monologue went something like this: "'Okay, let's do it,' that means let's get married, right? Oh my God, it is actually happening. I don't want to sound eager and I need to tread lightly in case I misunderstood. I also don't want to drag this out, I've already waited eight years, that's enough."

He had meant that we should get married. The next decision was to pick a date. "Three is our favorite number, so we should get married in March, the third month of the year." I absolutely was not waiting an entire year, so this month it was.

For the day, there were only two options, since we made the actual decision that three's were it, either the thirteenth or the thirty-first. The number sequence that we liked the best was 313. The hard part was done, we had decided to get married and picked the date. There was never a thought about having an actual wedding. He's too cheap to spend money on something "frivolous" like a wedding.

I made the phone call to my parents first while we were stopped at the gas station filling up the 350Z on that same drive home from Costco.

"Hey, sweetie!"

"Hi, Mom! Is Daddy with you?"

"Yeah, we are both here. Is everything okay?"

"Oh yeah. Soooooo, Lovie and I are getting married."

"Oh, honey, congratulations!" There was some hesitation in Mom's voice.

"Thanks, it just happened. We have picked a date. Since we both love threes, we chose March 13."

"Oh, wow. Okay, so March 13 of next year. Do you think y'all are going to do a big wedding?"

"No, Mama, March 13 this year. In like ten days. We're just gonna go to the courthouse in Georgia. We are moving into the new house anyway that weekend."

(Stunned silence before she sweetly continued) "Oh. Okay. So, will anyone be there with y'all? And why Georgia again?"

"Remember us telling you that his mom just moved up there? We figured it would be nice, especially since I know there is no way anyone on my side can come on such short notice. That's also where my besties are, and I want them there. Plus, there is a longer waiting period here in Florida. I love the 313 date and with the move already set that weekend, logistically it makes sense to do it all at the same time. It's a sign that everything lined up so nicely."

"That's right, I do remember that. Well, honey, we are happy for you."

Yes, ten days was fast but other than asking off work that Monday, there was no need for planning. I found a dress for $30 at Ross, I bought him a $17 ring from Amazon, a $20 white button-down shirt to wear with his khaki pants, and a $10 temporary band at Walmart for me. I loved that cheap ring because it's the one he slid on my finger. But inevitably, it turned my finger green.

The guest list was short: JR was my Maid of Honor whose job was to hold the phone for my parents to watch on FaceTime, Boo was his Best Woman, and Tiffy and Mama V were there. That was it. We all showed up at the courthouse on Monday afternoon to stand in front of a judge with ten other couples we'd never met before. He smiled and made sweet jokes throughout and when it was over; we went to a reception dinner where the littles in our life joined us. It was simple and everything was perfect.

I knew going in that his main reason for getting married to me was initially for my financial gain. He is always looking for ways to invest, increase capital and save money, so working would never be an issue. Getting legally married was a smart financial decision. He was also investing in us as a couple. Going in front of a judge was his way of saying, "I am making a commitment to make us work." He knew how much I wanted to be legally married because it was what I had grown up aspiring to. Outside of the romantic ideals of marriage, being legally married meant that we were partners in the eyes of the legal system. We could use that to build a life: buying houses or getting loans with financing, filing taxes every year, etc.

I am a hopeless romantic in theory. I watch too many Hallmark movies. A fun fact that surprises most people, I am uncomfortable verbally expressing my emotions or hearing someone else express them to me. Regardless of how elated I was that we were actually saying vows to each other, it was pretty awkward for me to repeat what the judge was saying. I felt every single word in my soul but saying them out loud, even in a low whisper, was uncomfortable.

It was years later that I recognized the discomfort in saying and hearing loving words comes from insecurity and lack of love for myself. The day of our wedding, Lovie did not say his vows out loud. He leaned his forehead against mine and maintained eye contact through the entire thing while shaking his head yes but never said a word out loud. I knew in my heart he was agreeing, he felt the words he was not repeating but was not ready to speak them aloud.

I kept this detail to myself for a couple of years. When I shared it with my besties, they seemed taken aback. He didn't say the vows? Didn't that upset me? Truthfully, it did not. I knew that he loved me and was doing the one thing he said he'd never do again, just to make me smile. Get married. I didn't need to hear him repeat what a stranger was telling him to know that he was committing himself to me. I knew that in his own way, he would show me and eventually, he would express his love in his own style.

Those first couple of days after we were married were beyond paradise. I'd open my eyes and there he was leaning over me with a huge grin. "Good morning, My Wife." Moving past me in the bathroom, he would put his hands on my hips, "Hubby coming through." We couldn't keep our hands off each other the entire week. Sadly, I knew it couldn't last more than this week. We didn't live together. Once he left for South Florida, the spell would be broken.

I was still not allowed to be at the farm; Pandora had forbidden it and doubled down on her stance when he told her we were married. He didn't tell her beforehand so she couldn't create drama to ruin our bliss. She continued pushing to be more than friends with benefits and they shared a home. The last thing I wanted to think about on my wedding day was her; I wanted his head 100 percent in the happiness of our celebration. The fact was, us being married, was not going to stop her from trying to be with him. I can't fault her for trying based on two reasons.

One, we were going to have to figure out what being married looked like for us at this stage of our lives. The primary consideration: We did not live together and logistically that wasn't going to be possible for the foreseeable future. My job required me to live in Georgia and while I was on the road more often than not, my boss wouldn't allow me to home base from Florida. Lovie was not leaving the farm.

We would continue the fourteen hundred-mile loop in order to see each other. The goal was never to go more than two weeks, but reality was that marriage wasn't going to affect our current travel routine and that was a long commute. Dating separately was not an option for me. As committed partners, any outside relationship would have to work for both of us, not just be accepted by one of us (me, I'm the "us"). My FOMO is entirely too strong. I knew I'd never be okay with him dating. He agreed he wanted the same. However, Lovie having the freedom to play with others was non-negotiable. He was not willing to give up an opportunity because I was not there. This was not my favorite, but it was what it was. Sex can be just sex.

The second reason I can't fault Pandora for trying to keep a relationship alive, he was still an active and willing participant. I couldn't stop him and wasn't going to ask. Having sex with her was convenient, just across the living room. There was no chase, no effort required, and it was familiar. I was proving that being married would not change his routines, that our new label didn't come with new restrictions. My goal was to let him fly, never cage him in. If I was nonchalant about it, why wouldn't she keep trying?

I approached most hard conversations thinking I was a "burden." If I asked him not to play with our ex-girlfriend, he might think I was nagging. Even worse, maybe he would change his mind, decide I was too much work and ask for a divorce. Not a healthy way for me to approach marriage. It was my responsibility to be clear about how I felt when he was intimate with her. Boundaries were never redefined. I did express my dislike of the situation, but how did I present it? It was more of a question than a statement. I was meek, unsure how to express my deepest feelings, and I never said, "This hurts me." No matter how nonchalantly I expressed concern though, when he kept on, that was on him. He made a conscious choice to push that envelope.

What I was verbalizing to him and what I was venting about to my besties got jumbled in my mind. I was so worried about *appearing* to be cool that I may not have fully expressed all my thoughts to him. No person is a mind reader, and it's unrealistic to assume everything you say is exactly what they hear. Saying the same thing three different ways can be necessary. I needed to figure out a more effective way to communicate, explaining how my heart got tiny cracks when he shared those stories of being with Pandora.

They continued sleeping together, not frequently but enough to irritate me. Each time got harder for me even because his commitment to us grew each day. "I love you" was said more often. He missed me, and he made more efforts to shorten our time apart. He was showing me in all ways, except this one thing, that he'd fallen in love with me. Eventually, I realized she was not the issue. My view switched over to him. I became more hurt when I made this connection, he knew I was uncomfortable yet kept doing it. Pandora was not in our marriage; she was not the one responsible to do right by me. He was. She didn't have to give two shits how I felt. He did.

Every time we hung up after he'd called to tell me details, I was a blubbering mess. Boo cradled my head on the sofa and told me it was okay and listened to me sob about a situation I had signed up for. And agreed to. She saw the toll this arrangement took on me and then had to watch me minimize it to him. October of 2018, I broke down on the phone and said I couldn't hurt like this anymore. My pain threshold showed itself physically, and I finally expressed, through controlled sobs, how deeply this hurt me. I was so hurt because they had intimate experiences together. It hurt me that his voice was numb when answering my questions. It hurt most that a year and a half later, we were still having this conversation. That was the last time Pandora and Lovie were ever together. I asked him later what made that the last time. "I saw how much it hurt you and it wasn't worth it to me." In December of 2018, after a year and a half living apart, we made the leap. I packed up my things in Georgia and moved into the farmhouse.

CHAPTER 12

SHINY COMMITMENTS

"Love recognizes no barriers. It jumps hurdles, leaps fences, penetrates walls to arrive at its destination full of hope."
— Maya Angelou —

We vacationed in Washington state for the Fourth of July 2017. We'd been married for four months, and this was the first time going to see my mom, dad, and sisters. My family has always been close and their acceptance of him was paramount. I wanted them to witness how he always opens doors, immediately stops whatever he's doing if I call his name, and to see firsthand what a good man he is. They needed to see us interact to understand how much good there is between us and why I refused to give up on our relationship. As expected, we had a blast, and we planned to come back out for Christmas.

My original engagement ring was a lab-created sapphire stone in a sterling silver setting that he got from Jared, online for $99. The original picture showed small diamonds around the halo; that image was zoomed in ... a lot. The tiny specks of diamond dust were barely visible. I loved that ring because it was unique, and the center stone was over one carat. I've always been a fan of big, gaudy jewelry and this ring definitely had the size. As beautiful as it was, I was pushing for something bigger because I like sparkly things. We had been investing for several years and Lovie told me that if our investments hit a certain amount, he would replace my ring with real diamonds. I was watching it every single day.

2017 was a phenomenal year for investment and by the beginning of December, it looked like we might actually hit the target. While I was in New Orleans at a work conference, I found a way to make a plug for a big Christmas gift in every conversation that week. He laughed me off each time, saying, "We'll see." Then his response changed mid-week when he laughed and said, "Go ahead and start looking at different settings." We hadn't quite hit that target price yet, but I knew he wouldn't mess with me on something like this; it was actually happening.

A major snowstorm hit the Southeast, and we weren't able to get out of New Orleans. With the conference over and flights cancelled, two friends and I went to Jared to look at rings and kill some time. I wanted a replica of what he had originally given me, with real diamonds around a genuine sapphire stone. I found the most gorgeous setting and sent him the information.

My conference days start way earlier than he wakes up so typically we text good morning and talk later in the day. I was surprised the next morning when my phone rang and his face popped up. He'd called instead of texted because he was actually at the Jared store. His big question: Did I want a sapphire or diamond as the middle stone? Lovie is above frugal. When he said the stones were about the same price and I could decide which one I wanted, I questioned it. I asked multiple times if he was sure the stones were the same price because, in my experience, diamonds are way more expensive. If given a choice between a diamond or a stone, I'm going to choose diamonds—duh. But this was different. I ultimately decided I wanted a ring that looked like my original.

It wasn't a surprise gift, somehow it was better. I knew that when he flew into Atlanta so we could fly together to Seattle, I would be receiving the best gift ever. I tried to play it cool but I was bouncing like a five-year-old on Christmas morning. I scooped him from the airport and, since he was starving, we stopped on the way home to get a Publix sub. Oh, my lord, the waiting was torture. The entire time he sat casually at the kitchen table, eating his sandwich at the slowest speed ever, I stared at his backpack. I knew my present was in there. Boo was sitting with us, and they both laughed at how fidgety I was. The moment he finished chewing the last bite, I had to ask. I could not wait another second. He grinned and reached into his backpack.

It was perfect. Boo was there with us, he walked over to me, got on one knee, opened the box, and said, "Will you continue to be my wifey forever?" This was the first time someone had ever proposed to me. We never talked about any proposal, he just remembered that was my dream. The love I felt in that moment overflowed from my eyes.

Then I ruined it.

When he opened the box, the ring had fallen forward so when he handed it to me it wasn't upright. My response, like a giant dingbat, was, "Try again," and gently pushed the box back toward him.

What the fuck? Who says that? Try again?

I did, I said that.

His laugh washed away my immediate fear: I'd ruined the most romantic moment of my life. He repositioned the ring and opened it again. I was stunned. In that tiny box was the most beautiful diamond center stone in the setting that I had picked out. My first thought was "wait ... this isn't the sapphire I wanted". Thank God that was just in my mind and not said out loud. Then I proceeded that it was a DIAMOND. Oh, my god. It was incredible. This man had spent a massive amount of money, just to make me happy, to show his commitment to me. That was the exact day I knew he was in love with me for the rest of our lives.

Three is my favorite number. I am one of three sisters; I have three aunts who are like mothers to me, I have always had a posse of three best friends. And I believe that three is the number of people that make up my perfect relationship. When he handed me the paperwork, I was floored. "Did you do this on purpose?" His blank stare told me told the answer.

The halo diamonds were a total carat weight of 1.33 and the center stone was 2.03 for a total carat weight of 3.36. It literally could not get any better. I was floating for the rest of the evening. I couldn't stop staring at my finger. Not only did I have the biggest and most beautiful ring I could imagine, but Lovie had gotten on one knee to propose with Boo there for all of it. I had so much love coursing through my body, I thought I might actually burst.

Now that I had officially been proposed to, I was curious about his past proposals. He had been married once before we met and then was engaged to Pandora. I was utterly shocked by his response to this question. I knew his first marriage was a matter of timing and convenience, so it wasn't surprising there was no formal engagement or proposal. What did throw me for a loop was his recollection of the engagement to Pandora.

According to his account of that anniversary evening back in 2012, they had gone to dinner and walked on the beach. She'd been talking about getting engaged for some time and he wanted to give her what she was asking for, so there was a conversation. He said she mentioned that she only wanted to get married when she was at an ideal weight to him. He had not, as she described to me, made a grand gesture in getting on one knee and professing his undying love for her. The first and only time he had ever gotten on one knee and proposed to any woman was me, in the kitchen at the Kennesaw house on December 19.

I was shocked. SO many thoughts went through my head about the deception and the falsehoods that she told me. I questioned why he did not correct her when he heard her telling me the story. But it all lies in the past.

This one conversation sparked many questions more about our previous life experiences and what else I was incorrectly told.

Could I have chosen to be upset? Yes.

Could I have called into question every motive and action he had in the past? Yes.

But what would be the point? Our triad relationship was one based on lies, partial truths, and deception.

Everything that we went through brought us to where we are today. Our life, our commitment, has grown stronger because of the past. We've taken lessons she taught us about honesty and communication to use as our strength. Life is about learning, growing, and moving past obstacles in your path. Sometimes the more you struggle, the more you learn. And she might be our greatest lesson. From our first triad, we learned not only how to navigate rough water but also the joy having another woman in our life brings us both. We are Team Jolicoeur.

Today, over fourteen years later, every day is better than the last. We found how to create our paradise

Lovie, I loved you then, I love you now, I'll love you forever.

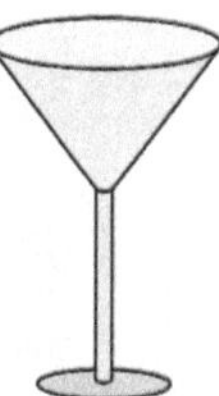

PART 2

CHAPTER 13

RELATIONSHIPS AND NEW CONCEPTS

*"Polyamory doesn't require a lack of jealousy,
but a willingness to take responsibility for one's feelings"*

It's important to talk about all things: relationship styles, guidelines, stereotypes, and sex. Not the actual ins and outs (pun intended) of sex, but the different ways it can be experienced in relationships.

As a general whole, society does not take kindly to things that are outside of the accepted "norm." This is why a cheating spouse in a monogamous relationship is socially accepted, but a faithful polyamorous one is "deviant." A co-worker of mine was married to a man that was repeatedly deceptive and unfaithful. We regularly had conversations about both our relationships, good, bad, indifferent, and the same questions were always asked. During drinks one night she asked me how I can be okay with my boyfriend (now husband) sleeping with other people and then emphatically added there was no way she could do it. I perceived judgment in her tone (or maybe it was the vodka) so I curtly respond, "The only difference between you and me is that I know where Lovie is, who he is with, and that he is being safe. Both partners are with other women, period."

For those partners who leave due to infidelity, I know how hard that is because I've done it. If you choose to forgive and forget each time, just be truthful with yourself that this will most likely not be the last time. The spouse who is cheating has a high probability of not being monogamously wired. Of course, there are some instances where it never happens again. But statistically, once someone cheats, they are three times more likely to cheat again. No, I did not make up that three-times figure to stay in my theme. It comes from research published in the *Archives of Sexual Behavior*, titled "Once a Cheater, Always a Cheater?" If you truly don't want to part ways with them, you may want to consider broadening your marriage guidelines to reduce the stress between you two. With enough communication, you have the ability to structure your life any way you desire.

I just said that some people are not monogamously wired. That is actually a thing. And to really blow your mind, many people believe that monogamy is actually unnatural. Now, that is not to say that monogamy is not possible. It totally is. Everyone knows at least one or two couples in their life, most likely parents or grandparents, who are monogamous, in love, and have never dealt with the heartbreaking event of infidelity during their long partnership.

I believe humans aren't meant to experience only one person sexually. I believe that you can have multiple soulmates. And yes, I believe that you can harmoniously love more than one person at a time. Does this mean I think all people in today's society are having to make a conscious choice to be monogamous and fight the urge to have multiple partners? No. It's more complicated.

We have become programmed to believe we should commit to one person for the rest of our lives and expect everything we need—emotionally, physically, and spiritually—should come from within ourselves and that other human. We are told not to look at anyone else for help (excluding doctors, priests, and therapists) because it would be a betrayal of our relationship.

When you start to break down what that actually means, it's a lot of responsibility.

Here's an example. I know women that get angry, not the playful angry but honestly mad when their partner stares or comments on another woman's appearance. Why do they get so angry? Do these women actually expect their men to only have eyes for them now? This seems like a ridiculous thing to fight about on two levels.

A) You are in public. He is not speaking a word to her as she walks by. He is not telepathically sending her the address to a hotel where they can meet for sex. Nope, he is simply staring at a visual that his brain said he liked. He's not blind.

2) Human appearances are artwork. No one gets mad at their partner for staring at a beautiful painting or sculpture. You are not buying it, not taking it home, but simply enjoying the beauty of what is in front of you. It's just not a realistic expectation for your partner to not find beauty outside of you.

But because it's another human, not an inanimate object, who has taken our lovers attention away from us, we feel our position has been temporarily threatened. This is because of our insecurities. Your partner staring at a supermodel doesn't mean they love you any less and certainly doesn't mean they find you unattractive. They are just appreciating something different. I know Lovie thinks I am beautiful. I also know that he finds lots of other shapes, sizes, skin tones, hair colors, and ethnicities beautiful as well. I love when he points out someone whom he finds attractive so we can share that brief experience together. Bottom line, I will never be taller, darker skinned, or any different shape. I can't change those factors. Being okay with your partner finding others attractive doesn't mean you're a swinger now. It means you're secure.

If you strip down all of your personal relationships to just the foundations, remove the labels we have placed on them, and look at the different dynamics, you might see traits of polyamory. You are probably shaking your head and completely disagreeing because you are thinking only about sex. Sex is not always the center of relationships and that's the hard part to process. We want everything in a pretty box, labeled for easy identification.

The best example I have, especially for women, is your best friend. Your best friend is the person you tell EVERYTHING to. You discuss major life events, support each other emotionally, vent about your partners/spouses, vacation together, lie in bed and watch TV, maybe even snuggle. You have a love for each other that is different from any other love in your life. Hopefully, these are all things you do with your partner too, just with the added bonus of sex.

When we were younger, most of lived with a person at some point who was not a sexual partner but fit every other check mark a spouse would. The most common label is roommate. You and your roommate cook meals together, get ready for parties in the same bathroom, binge Netflix while on the sofa, discuss money and budgets and talk about your sex lives.

I am not saying that you have a poly mindset just because you love your best friend. I'm attempting to show how multiple relationships already exist in our lives. Don't worry, honey, sleepovers with your bestie don't make you a Sister Wife. But it does show that you have the capacity to love more than one person. This is a step toward understanding that polygamy, polyamory, and swinging are not that far out of the social norm.

For centuries, native cultures of the world have based their entire civilization around the community being one family, the literal meaning of "it takes a village." Men were the providers, hunting, trapping, trading, and making sure every member of the tribe had a place to eat and sleep. Women were responsible for taking care of the children, cooking, clothing, and taking care of the man's needs. These men have sexual relationships with different women and then raise each woman's children as his own, regardless of paternity. They didn't worry about whose child is biologically whose. They all provided for each other to make sure each member of the village had the necessities to survive. This is not to say that there weren't some men and women who did not participate in this sexual behavior, I believe there most likely were. In today's society, you're no longer allowed to discuss gender roles, but centuries and centuries have survived with them as clear-cut job description.

Sex at Dawn: the Prehistoric Origins of Modern Sexuality, written by Cacilda Jetha and Christopher Ryan, is an intense read filled with an overwhelming amount of research regarding human sexuality, social structures, and how our present actions are pre-wired based on thousands of years of survival strategies. I believe these pre-wires are the base root of us and that over centuries our consciousness has evolved to allow for more individualized thinking and decision-making.

Look at the more "civilized" cultures from centuries long ago. Historically, kings, world leaders, royalty, and other wealthy men would have taken a wife and then had multiple other women as concubines or mistresses. The definition of a concubine is a woman who lives with a man but has a lower status than his wife or wives. A concubine is not a prostitute, although I'm sure many men enjoyed the company of ladies of the night as well.

Most women in earlier centuries weren't given a choice to be in a "polyamorous" life and were just forced to do so because that was the societal norm for that time. That was how things were done. People simply did not marry for love. Families married off their daughters for survival, money, political gain, or control. The teenage daughter was often pimped out for the best interest of the family name. One of my favorite shows, *The Tudors*, was especially eye-opening to me because of the nothing-is-off-limits approach in showcasing customs of Europe during the fifteenth century. The life and wives of

Henry VIII were the centerpiece. Up to that point, I only knew the romanticized, fairy-tale versions of old England. Watching this show is what got me interested in how marriage and politics were so closely entwined. It had never entered my consciousness that marriage was about anything more than love and being together forever.

It was a very dark story from these times, how women were viewed as commodities used for political gain and to bear sons. Ironically, if a woman gave birth to a daughter, she had failed her husband. Women were faithful to men who cheated on them, fathered children outside of their marriage, ignored them, and generally viewed them as useless and there wasn't anything they could do about it. They were expected to stay home, raise children, and accept their fate.

Keep in mind, this was not just done in one country, and it was not always under duress. The Greeks, French, Romans, Egyptians, and many others joined the English in these practices. If a man could afford multiple wives and could provide a good life for them, the more the merrier. Women often found comfort in knowing that the happiness of the husband and security of the family did not rest solely on her shoulders. Families would enter into polyamorous marriages for survival since more people meant more land and resources.

Getting married for love is a relatively new concept. It was not until the eighteenth or nineteenth centuries that the idea of getting married simply because you were in love even came about. During early centuries, getting married for love was considered a mental illness and meant you could be disowned by your family, according to Stephanie Coontz in her book, *Marriage, A History: How Love Conquered Marriage*. Many spouses did happen to fall in love with each other once married, but that was a happy side effect.

Swinging, polyamory, and open marriages are not new to American society even though they've been taboo. Our country has a long-standing history of what was known as the "free love movement" that started in the nineteenth century and gained some traction from 1915 to 1925 in trendy parts of New York City. Following World War II, Key Clubs or Key Parties started popping up. These parties were known for wife swapping and got their name because a key was required to enter the buildings. This concept grew through the 1950s, spreading out to house parties and more organized clubs which became popular across the US and even in traditional suburbs. From there, the hippies of the 1960s launched that free-love movement to the next level.

According to a study in the EJHS, "The concept of having more than one loving relationship at a time also made its debut in the sixties and may be responsible for the sexual philosophy active in many hippie communities of the time." The 1970s get credit for the birth of the word swinging—I guess wife-swapping started to sound too sexist.[1]

I struggled with putting things into defined buckets when writing because there is no way to incorporate every point of view. The thing about life, nothing is ever simplistic. Especially when dealing with sensitive subjects like love and sex. There will always be more gray than black and white, so keep that in the forefront of your mind as you read on.

Humans love labels. We need them to be able to wrap our heads around something that is beyond our construct of understanding. The amount of stereotypes around different relationships is never ending.

Take monogamy. This is a seemingly simple concept to explain, two humans committed to only love and make love with each other. Where this gets gray is in *how* each relationship is structured. Some couples choose to do everything together. These are the couples that have a hard time going out without each other and, when they do, are texting constantly. If you are in a monogamous relationship where you and your partner

---

[1] https://askwonder.com/q/statistics-demographics-and-size-of-the-life-style-swinger-market-57daf90faec4161a008a7d8f)

are living two separate lives, the aforementioned structure will seem smothering and may signal a lack of trust. Judgment made. On the flip side, the couple who lives separate lives may seem that they aren't in love or don't want to spend time together because they are frequently apart. Judgment made. The same applies to poly relationships.

General terminology defines a polyamorous relationship as one that has more than two people in a committed romance. You can have two women and one man, two men and one woman, three men, three women, two men and two women, three women and one man. You get the idea.

You could have a V, where one person is the "point" of the other two people. Imagine there is a dot on each end of that V. The bottom dot is in a relationship with both lines but those two are not romantically involved. You have couples, or groups of couples, who are committed to each other. The most commonly known form of poly is the triad, which is what Lovie and I identify with.

Polyamory is a life commitment that's about family, building a foundation, and of course, great sex. Swinging is more about sexual experiences and friendships versus building a life together.

A couple years after we got married, Lovie and I met a couple at the club and we hit it off right away. The four of us started spending lots of time together; it was perfect. We went to nice restaurants, partied at the Hard Rock Casino, and had game nights at their house.

For a year and a half, the four of us had an epic connection and our communication was always on point. We had clear boundaries (or lack thereof) and when The Husband and I fell asleep early, there was no issue if The Wife and Lovie wanted to keep playing. Since we did not have the time to date to find our potential life partner, this dynamic was a dream come true for us. We got vanilla time with friends and chocolate time with playmates that we were completely comfortable with.

Somewhere along the line, the dynamic started to shift, slowly. There started to be some personality differences between me and The Wife but nothing dramatic. Then one day, she pulled Lovie and me aside to ask, "Are we not enough?"

This was out of left field because we never hid the fact we were still going to the club and enjoying the swinging lifestyle, but we apparently were not explicit with that information. "Are we not enough?" is a question you might ask a romantic partner. It certainly implies a level of intimacy. We were not in a relationship with them, but she felt some kind of way after she went digging into our online profiles for information.

She had gone onto our SDC account and saw we went to Trapeze the night after hanging out with them. Her line of questions indicated that she thought the four of us were in a relationship, not just great friends with benefits. She had drilled down to see a couple we had validated from that night, which is a feature on the website, and assumed that each couple we validated, we'd slept with. Not accurate. Validation is simply a way to indicate you have met the person/s and their profile is an honest representation.

Even after explaining we validate *all* profiles we meet in person, to confirm they are real and looked like their pictures, she kept questioning why they weren't enough. Then she moved into asking why we hung out with "ugly" or "fat" people. That was a hard line for me. Beauty is relative but every human has beauty. I have never, and will never, narrow down who I talk with, laugh with or communicate with simply because of physical appearance. To be clear, outward attraction is very important to me when it comes to hook-ups. But what I find beautiful and what you find beautiful might be two completely different images. Just because we are poly/swingers/lifestyle does not mean that if we talk to you, we want to sleep with you. Friendships are just as important.

Shortly after that, we parted ways. I saw her as a "mean girl", I felt uncomfortable with her comments and did not like the direction this was going. There was no fight, no breakup. We just drifted apart, and then COVID happened and time got away.

Boo has something she calls a "rerun." I giggled out loud when she said it because I had an inkling what it was but had never actually heard it used. A rerun is a relationship that has ended for fundamental reasons, but you continue to try again when nothing has changed from before. It's literally the same episode, on a different day. A rerun is just trying again for a different outcome, but the possibility of change isn't there.

We did a rerun with The Husband and The Wife. We all started hanging out again about a year later. I was never honest about the reason we originally dropped off because I don't know how to tell someone it's their personality that sucks. I figured I might be in a different head space now and maybe I'd been too harsh in my judgments.

After a couple weeks, they shared that their marriage dynamic had shifted. The Husband was starting to court someone new and while he wanted to hang out with us, he did not want to play anymore out of respect for this new love interest. Totally fair. My breaking point on this go-round was the lack of respect from The Wife on how Lovie and I structure our relationship.

They had chosen to try an open marriage, where both are able to have outside relationships from each other. They communicated and agreed to their boundaries and kept it moving. Lovie and I are poly, currently enjoying the swinger lifestyle, but we are not open. We have agreed to do everything together. I have no interest in a marriage where my husband has external relationships that I am not involved in. My FOMO is too strong. There is absolutely nothing wrong with open relationships, it is just not for me. I know my jealousy would be on ten. I know myself well enough to know I could not emotionally handle that; I need to be involved.

The Wife thought my boundary was dumb and it showed I

was a jealous person. I have always been one hundred percent upfront that external relationships are not for me. She began to stay up later and later, well after The Husband and I went to sleep, and then wanted to play with just Lovie. She began to have secret conversations with him and would get quiet when I came around. To quote Lovie, "She made it really obvious she wanted relationship with just me."

One morning after The Husband and I had both fallen asleep earlier than them, I asked if anyone played, and she quickly replied "no" to which Lovie agreed. We all got ready for the day, enjoyed a lovely breakfast with fantastic coffee and then parted ways. Not two seconds after we got in the car to drive home, Lovie said, "I don't know why she said that, she gave me head." I was livid. Livid at the fact that she was deceitful, but even more mad at Lovie for lying to me.

He should have spoken up the moment she answered no and said, "Yeah, we did." His reasoning for not saying anything was to avoid any issues between The Husband and The Wife just in case she wasn't going to tell her husband. Wrong answer. I took this as an act of loyalty to her and protecting her by being deceptive toward me. To his credit, Lovie did tell me the moment we were alone and we were able to hash out that if a similar situation ever occurs later, tell me first thing. I view withholding information in this scenario the same as lying.

I did text The Wife and address the issue immediately. We worked out the semantics of wording and agreed to be more specific in the future. I felt good that I spoke up, got uncomfortable in a conversation and then was okay to move on. One statement she made stuck with me though, "I don't know why you are all upset anyway, it was just head." This type of belittling is unacceptable. No one gets to tell you how you should feel about any sexual situation. When you're sharing partners, sharing energy, and having intimate experiences with other people's spouses, you must respect ALL boundaries they have.

It could be different each time. That might get frustrating, but as long as everyone is communicating what they need, you have agreed to those standards by continuing to participate. If you do not agree with or don't like the rules, you need to leave. It is not the responsibility of the other party to change their boundaries.

After one last attempt to spend time together, she sent me a long text message saying that we needed to part ways because of my jealousy and that she was not the only one who noticed. My insecurities had caused too much discomfort for her. She said I had changed the rules of the game. She wrote that they felt bad for Lovie and wished the three of them might be able to maintain a friendship.

My response was that I would not defend myself or my marriage and wished them well. My rules never changed. We were still poly, just enjoying swinging. I never wavered on the fact that we do everything together, there's nothing separate. This highlights the judgment within the lifestyle community. Everyone believes their way is the right way. Since they chose to open up their marriage, The Wife automatically assumed that we should follow suit. If I have not mentioned it before, Lovie made several comments to me over those weeks about how he noticed she was trying to pull him away and had made several comments about the two of them dating without me. I was not willing to change my mind and send Lovie off on one-on-one dates, so now I was a jealous, overbearing wife in her mind. I am okay if that is what her perception is. It's not totally incorrect. I was envious. Her reason though was very wrong. I was not jealous because I thought Lovie was more into her than me. I was not jealous because she was prettier than me (she was so beautiful when she smiled). I was envious because I was intentionally being left out of a party that I wanted to participate in.

What I ultimately want out of life is a closed triad where we all live happily ever after in love. This is a process though;

it does not happen overnight. Especially when it took eight years for Lovie and I to get to the marriage level.

I have a favorite lesbian joke: What does a lesbian bring on a second date?

A U-Haul.

I laugh every time because it has a level of accuracy to it that I can personally give multiple examples to illustrate. I am one of those examples. I meet my ex-wife, spent the night once and never really left again. It can be easy for me to go from zero to one hundred when clicking with a new soul.

Lovie and I have figured out the best way for us to navigate meeting new people. When we meet a woman we're both interested in on a digital platform, Lovie will reach out and start the conversation. I'm horrible with conversation starters online or through texting. I also don't have the patience for mundane small talk. If the conversation moves along and there are common interests, he will bring me into the communication thread. While all the communication is happening, Lovie show's me every text and keeps me in the loop. I thrive when there is personal connection, like in-person meetings and phone calls, so I initiate those. If there is any excitement building for either of us, we will invite her out, usually for drinks with the open-ended invite for dinner if things go well. Initial physical attraction must be mutual for us, but our levels of engagement can be varied; one of us might be super pumped and the other one may be luke-warm.

Many times, that initial infatuation with a new love interest is intense. You relish the idea of spending as much time as possible together. It might have to do with an amazing sexual connection you experienced right at the start, or it might be the *anticipation* of a sexual connection in the future, once you get better acquainted.

Humans often link other emotions to lust. Sex releases endorphins and makes you feel emotionally high. Sex is an exchange of energies. It's easy to let the "feel goods" take over.

But it's not always about lovemaking. The old saying, "When two people really love each other ..." doesn't have to apply. Love and sex are not mutually exclusive.

After the initial infatuation calms down, dating begins. This looks like hours spent on the phone, drinks, Facetime calls and dinners out. This period of time could last months or years. The pandemic made this part difficult because restaurants were closed down, people were (and some still are) scared to be around people outside their bubble.

I want a partnership that has a solid foundation. Truthfully, I get gun-shy when Lovie mentions finding "a wife." I am skittish about that because I need to know we've worked up to that stage. I don't want to move too quickly and let infatuation cloud paradise. Slow and steady will win the race. Once everyone falls into a comfortable dynamic of dating, life just begins to flow, and we can blissfully move forward.

Lovie and I have dated some in our six years as a married team, but nothing has progressed past that. The difficulty in finding a new partner is finding someone who fits into our dynamic, someone who is open to loving us equally and wants to commit to a family. It's easier for us because we already have an established love so it's only one new person to date. However, on the other side, she has two people to learn about and examine feelings for. This is especially difficult for people who are new to the lifestyle because transitions from a monogamous mind set to a polyamorous one can have many switchbacks. There might be moral questions you wrestle with if you came from a religious upbringing. You could think about jealousy, doubt your ability to have the capacity to love two people at once, or stress over what your family and friends might say.

Believe me, navigating telling your family that you are not "traditional" or trying not to tell them too much is a bitch. It's really hard sometimes. My family follows the "don't ask questions you don't want answers to" rule. My parents love and support any decision I make. However, we've never been a family that shares deeply intimate details about our lives. They know we are poly, I know they know and they know I know they know. It works for us. When we find a partner who seamlessly fits into our life, we will have deeper conversations with my family about our commitment to each other. Until then, I have no desire to talk about our sex life with my mom or dad. On the flip side, Lovie's family knows every detail. Poor Mama V was broken in super early.

One of the primary reasons I am hesitant jump into a "wife" label is because in the last twenty years, research has been done to show how human personalities change over time. A quick internet search shows a general consensus that we experience these changes every seven to ten years. An article on npri.com from June 2013 cited Harvard research, that humans can recognize how they have changed from their past but don't see that they will continue to change in the future. Basically, we become a new person every seven to ten years. This is where the idea of the seven-year itch comes from because we learn new things and need to spread our wings. In relationships you must grow together, or you will grow apart.

Another nrp.com article from June 2016 explains our "Big Five" traits that change are Extraversion (characterized by adjectives like outgoing, assertive, and energetic versus quiet and reserved); agreeableness (compassionate, respectful, and trusting versus uncaring and argumentative); conscientiousness (orderly, hard-working, and responsible versus disorganized and distractible); negative emotionality (prone to worry, sadness, and mood swings versus calm and emotionally resilient); and open-mindedness (intellectually curious, artistic, and imaginative versus disinterested in art, beauty, and abstract ideas). While these traits don't seem to change at the core, how we handle them does change as we get older. Because you don't see changes in people overnight, it is important to put in the time together to ensure compatibility.

When that growth happens together, then we can talk about

the next step in our relationship. Is that moving in together if we have not already? Is that a commitment ceremony? Who knows. Is it possible that we will find the partner who is perfect for us and things just happen quickly, causing all my best-laid plans to be thrown out the window? Absolutely. You don't get to pick how and when your relationship will develop. We all know one couple that meet from a one night stand, moved in together after two weeks and were married within a few months. Statistically they will not make it but some do. I believe some things are just kismet but most need time.

It is easy to write out and think I am in control of the future. One important life lesson I have learned: I am exactly where I should be in this moment. Each laugh, heartache, uncomfortable conversation, and each kiss was meant for that exact time.

CHAPTER 14

COMMUNICATION

*"Good communication is the bridge between
confusion and clarity"*
— Nat Turner —

This is one of my favorite subjects to talk about. I am beyond passionate about it because it is the sole reason fights, arguments and misunderstandings occur. **It's not what you say; it's how you say it.** I have yet to find a situation that wouldn't have gotten a better outcome if all parties involved were more aware of their tone and more selective with their words.

Everyone communicates in different ways. It's part of what makes us unique. I believe that part of the human experience is learning how to be effective with your words and body language so you can make a difference in someone's life, even if that someone is yourself. There are over 7.5 billion people on planet Earth, and we have conversations with at least five to ten different people each day, more if you work in an office or retail environment. Some of these exchanges are just basic pleasantries while checking out at the grocery store or placing a coffee order in a cafe. We seem to focus our attention more on the longer conversations we have with our partners, friends, and co-workers that we may not realize that with good communication, every interaction will be beneficial, even in brief encounters.

Think about the last time you had a rough day and went to order a coffee from a complete stranger at your favorite coffee spot. The barista asked how your day was going. How did you react? Did you A) immediately go off and rant about how shitty your day has been going, B) ignore the question altogether and just snarl back, or C) answer "fine" and walk away to wait for your drink? Most of us would answer "fine," give a fake smile and move on to the end of the bar. We feel that the person behind the bar is *required* to ask about your day and is on autopilot. (Funny story: Lovie plays a game with people when they ask, "How are you?" He responds, "Another day in paradise. How about you?" And then counts how many times they repeat the same question, and the circle continues. So far, the longest count has been three cycles before the person realized they had been repeating themselves.) Anyway, then you get home and your husband/wife/kids asks the same question: How was your day? Do we say "fine" and walk away like with the barista earlier in the day? Oh, hell no. We immediately launch into everything negative that happened today, all the ways other people wronged us, and probably throw in some random things that are completely irrelevant but just feel right to bring up ... right now.

Sometimes, you feel better after you vent, get a hug, and then can move on because all you needed was that quick minute. Happy ending. Or the opposite could happen. This scenario is what we want to avoid at all costs. This is when bad things happen.

I say a lot of things when I am angry, hurt, or have just received news that is hard to digest. It is kind of like a stream of consciousnesses while I struggle to find words and put thoughts together, so random stuff comes out of my mouth. I am definitely a processor. Depending on the topic, I tend to go to the most extreme place possible. Most of the words I say in that exact second I mean, but give me another minute to process and I most likely have changed my mind. As it sinks in, I start to creep back toward the rational and logical side. Sounds crazy, but I bet if you take a minute to reflect on your initial reactions, you can probably relate. It is because of this, Lovie and I started using the five-minute rule.

The five-minute rule is pretty simple. Anything I say in the first five minutes cannot be used against me in this argument or any future discussion and is not to be taken as my stance on a given topic. I can say with utmost certainty that he has honored this rule, and this is a HUGE reason we communicate as well as we do. The golden key to making this work is having all partners agree to this one staple rule. If all parties do not agree or buy in, it won't work. Simply saying you won't hold it against each other is not good enough. You must show and prove that you mean it; there must be trust. There have been times I have wanted to bring up something he has mentioned or said, and I have to remind myself that past is past—move forward.

While I don't consider our relationship to be an open marriage, both of us have the ability and freedom to play outside as long as there is not an ongoing relationship. In the first year and a half of our marriage, he chose to exercise this right. I chose to only play with others when we were together; that was solely my choice. Many assume that there was a double standard that he could play with others, and I could not. This is not true. The reasons I chose not to look for other playmates were time and energy. I did not have a desire to cultivate any new friendship. It's a lot of work and between Lovie, my family, friends, career, and taking care of myself, there is no spare time. Since the fall of 2018, however, we naturally evolved into a groove that put us in a new space in our relationship. Neither one of us have individual play friends. The option is still there of course but we have had many, many, many loving conversations in which both of us expressed a desire to be a complete team on everything, including sex and relationships. I think this is important to know as I explain more about how the five-minute rule has and will be applied to me. Your five-minute rule may look quite different—that's excellent. This is wonderful news because it means that you took a concept and made it fit your individual relationship.

Another part of our five-minute rule is that we must disclose anything that the other would think is a big deal immediately the next time we talk to each other; i.e, playing with someone else, large financial purchases, or potential impact on the other's life. My preference was (and still is if that occasion arose) that I know beforehand if an opportunity came up for him to play with someone new so I can mentally prepare myself for any of the questions I may or may not want to ask.

The five-minute rule came about when he would play with Pandora and tell me about it after the fact when he would finally answer his phone or text after an all-night party with her. This did not go over well in the beginning of our re-connection OR first part of our marriage. I was so hurt, so angry, and so annoyed all at the same time. I had so many emotions swirling around inside that the best answer I could give myself on how to deal with all of them was just to walk away from the relationship. I couldn't handle this dynamic. I was not being dramatic; the feeling gets worse each time, and I would tell myself I won't compete with her anymore. It would take me various amounts of time to process how I felt after each event. Every single time, I realized as I took my five or so minutes/hours, that I could in fact do this and that I still wanted to; I just needed to figure out how to effectively communicate to him why his actions affected me the way they did.

Now is a good time to speak to the "compete" comment I just made. I spent many, many years comparing myself to other women. They are prettier, smarter, thinner, more fun than me. I would try to be sexier, but I just felt silly. I tried to be more intellectual, but I would fumble and feel stupid; it's not who I am. I'm lighthearted, I watch the *Golden Girls* while I cross-stitch on Sunday mornings after partying all Saturday night at the swinger's club. I approach serious conversation with my "business" voice. I am excellent in a crisis, and I am the person you want planning the itinerary at Disney. I'm not the drunk party girl but I drink martinis like a 1930's flapper. I don't find vulgar humor funny but might die laughing telling a story about how I peed myself on a long run. I'm a walking contradiction. It's taken me almost forty years to stop competing and just be.

I cannot be more or less than I am. I still struggle with this, but the big realization came when I just stopped comparing Pandora and myself. We are nothing alike. Not physically, not emotionally, not spiritually. At the end of the day, if he wanted to be with her, then I could not make him happy and if he wanted my qualities in a partner, she could not make him happy. To use the analogy that hit this point home for me: You won't choose to eat an orange if you are craving an apple. They are not the same. No one else is me. Period. This is still a regular struggle for me: remember who you are. No one else can ever be that.

When Lovie would eventually call me to tell me about his nights, I usually began by asking questions, some of which I did not actually want the answer to. When he answered, I would just blurt out whatever came into my head. Sometimes, most times, I would start crying and repeat that I needed to process this, over and over, because I couldn't put any emotions or thoughts in actual words. He never held back any truth, and he was always patient, giving me my five minutes or waiting until I calmed down. After that first five, I was able to ask as many questions as I needed to. I could respond to his words in a level tone, and we were able to hang up feeling resolved and on track. This may take five minutes or five hours of conversation, but we put in the time immediately to handle it, so it does not come back up. That is the key: Handle any issue right then.

Obviously, there will be times when "right now" is not appropriate, like say at your parents' house for dinner or in the middle of a birthday party. But as soon as you are alone or in a place you can talk, start the conversation. Please start it calmly. It is also healthy to be able to know when you need a pause in the conversation. If things get out of hand, say you need a break and then come back. It's necessary to take care of your own emotions during these types of talks. Some words can never be taken back or forgotten. Take the emotional lap when you need it. (Thank you to Adrian Williams, for this living-changing advice.)

To this day, Pandora is the only thing we have had serious, heartbreaking conversations about. The best thing we ever did for us was to remove her from our lives. Sometimes, outside sources can be the reason you and your partners are not growing, thriving, or communicating. Because we were able to have these hard, uncomfortable conversations, we decided that it was time to sever all communication. Contrary to popular belief, I did not initiate the conversation of cutting all ties, it was Lovie. I'm going to paraphrase his words: He saw how much his actions were hurting me. He saw that our relationship and his freedom didn't change just because we got married. He only wanted to make me feel happiness. He had a shift in his view of her and the place she held in his life. He made the decision to completely break ties, I agreed, sat back, and watched his actions.

There is no topic restriction on the 5MR either. It applies to any major choices, heated discussion, argument, or any decision we have to make, big or small. True story: Lovie came to me one day and mentioned moving to Colombia, a country that is not stable and where we do not speak the language. Within two minutes, I had a gameplan for quitting my job and how many times a year we would visit family back in the States. Obviously, once I processed what this would mean, it became a little more complicated. But in that moment, I was all in. I have even evoked the rule when trying to decide if I want to watch a movie or play chess that night. It is not always a major decision, but it always allows me to process information and gives both of us the peace of mind that no situation is set in stone.

That is my favorite part of our communication. We are fluid. Communication should flow like a river, cheesy analogy, but it works perfectly. A river is always moving forward. Sometimes it is a smooth and slow ride, other times it is fast and rushing. There are parts that are treacherous with sharp rocks and logs rushing at anything in its path and you're really glad you have a life vest on. We have chosen, against all odds thrown at us thus far that we will stay in the raft and ride it out together. I can say at this moment, only three percent of our communication is negative or heated.

What do we fight about? Well, not the typical things. For us, sex and money are never an issue, financial situation maybe but never money. We have enough sex together and we have a balance of playtime with others that meets both of our needs. We have enough money, each with separate accounts and an even split on bills. What he does with his money outside of bills and household finance is his business. Annnnnd I fully expect that he never makes comments when our mailbox is overrun with Amazon packages. We had to work to get to this point as we are at complete opposite ends of the spending spectrum. I want a nice car and am a fan of name brands. I love shopping and when buying clothes, I generally don't ask myself "Do I need this?" I ask myself, "Do I have this already?" I find a brand that I become obsessed with (Skims and Peloton get all my money right now) and he chooses to wear a basic "uniform" every day from Walmart so he can invest every single penny possible.

After several years of back and forth, we settled on a compromise that works for us. I pay for things now and he is our retirement plan. Now, I totally get that this is not feasible for all couples, but it works for us. The main thing, in regard to finance, is to talk about what individual goals are and what the financial goals are for you as a couple. If one of you would be miserable giving up the $120 per month cable package or loves spending $100 on a bottle of wine, then keep that in your personal budget. Compromise is not always the answer; y'all may just agree to keep this these items separate from each other. Remember, you are two individual people, and you have two individual spending habits. You don't have to have a say in how the other spends money. Someone reading may be thinking, "Yeah, but I make more money so I get to say how it's spent." If that is what you and your partner talked about and agreed to, then that's your arrangement. But you will not have successful communication (or a success relationship) if one person is making all decisions, and the other is expected to just go with this. This builds resentment and ultimately causes walls to be constructed. That is the opposite of what we want. Knock those walls down. Say what you want. Keep this in mind: You get more flies with honey than vinegar. And don't spew years of frustration in one discussion.

As much as I know about communication and as much as I try to live out the things I teach, sometimes I just cannot understand him. I try to see both sides of the story, in particular, from his point of view. Can I put myself in his shoes? Does what I am saying make sense to his objections? I have mentioned this before, we usually only argue about financial decisions. Not money, financial decisions. Some of you are saying that it is the same thing and for some people it may be.

For me, the difference between financial decisions versus money is that money tends to revolve around the *amount* of cash, whereas financial decisions revolve around *how to spend* that cash. Some common disagreements around money might be the amount of credit card debt, overdraft fees on a bank account, borrowing money for one another, or other loaning issues. I generally find fights about money to have a common denominator, the lack of it. On the flip side, disagreements about financial decisions involve conversations on where to invest money, shopping habits, or how much to spend on vacations. That last one was the actual cause of a medium-sized disagreement between us.

In January of 2020, we had decided to take a quick three-night cruise while I was working in Fort Lauderdale so we could get a few extra points towards our Royal Caribbean Diamond status. Once you reach certain levels, the benefits provide you with some wonderful cost savings; two free photos and four free alcoholic drinks each are two of my favorites. It was worth it for me to pay for this trip. And that is where the argument began. What is worth it to me versus what is worth it to Lovie.

The room we had on that boat was a junior suite with a huge walk-in closet, actual bathtub instead of that teeny, tiny shower that I barely fit in, a comfortable lounging area, and spacious balcony. It was amazing. So, when our island adventure got canceled one day, we casually popped by the Next Cruise station to ask about a Transatlantic cruise. I had junior suites on my mind since I was loving every minute in the one we were in. The cruise we looked at was a thirteen-night adventure where we would be spending ten nights crossing the Atlantic Ocean and three nights between Spain and Rome. That's a lot of cruising nights and the idea of having so much space to really enjoy those ten days at sea sounded amazing. To top it off, the suite price was still $400 cheaper than our balcony room on an upcoming Bliss Cruise we already had booked—boom. I figured it was a slam-dunk sale. We got the price of an interior room, but that was really just to appease Lovie. Turns out, he had no intention of considering a balcony. It was the interior room or nothing.

While I was casually getting ready that afternoon, in our lovely, spacious suite room, we started to discuss the pros and cons of this European voyage.

I started the conversation by being cute and using my sweet voice.

"Babe, I've been itching to travel over to Europe *forever*.

We've always stayed in the Western Hemisphere; visiting all the Caribbean Islands, Mexico, Jamaica, and Colombia. I want to travel more of the world, I want to see different things, I want to experience different cultures."

(Lovie just nods his head, knowing I'm going to keep going.)

So, I continued, "Yes, the countries we've been to are all unique in their own way, but they have so many similarities that I am ready to branch out. You know how many times I have mentioned traveling to Europe in the last couple of years. I am so ready! Annnnd, can you imagine how amazing it will be to be at sea for ten nights in a junior suite with a balcony? We will have so much space."

He looked skeptical and replied, "Okay, so if you want to go to Europe, why don't we just get an interior room and save that extra money for another cruise? We can sit outside on the other decks. Why would we pay double the cost of an interior just to have more space; we could use that money to book a whole other cruise and it's still the same boat."

Getting annoyed, I responded, "Because it is about the experience of a suite! It's totally worth the money to upgrade when we're on such a long trip. This is twelve nights and thirteen days. It will be my first time to Europe and I want to be fancy. At some point walking the boat is gonna get old and I might want to see sunlight while having coffee in bed. I work really hard and if I want to spend my money on something like a beautiful suite on a cruise, it's totally worth it to me. This suite is *still* $400 cheaper than our Bliss cruise and it is for five more nights."

Then I added for sarcastic effect, "But you don't mind paying that price for Bliss because of the lifestyle experience, do you? I don't understand why this is such an issue for you. I will even cover the entire thing." At this point, I am fuming.

He either did not notice or did not care that I was upset and simply said, "It just doesn't make sense to pay that much for space that we don't need. It's a waste of money."

Red-faced, I responded, "How is me paying for a luxury, once in a lifetime experience, that I think will be incredible, a waste of money!? I know when we get there, we won't be doing fancy restaurants or bars, so I would like a bougie experience on the boat. Why is that such a bad thing?"

The next words he said calmly flowed out, "Because I'm not ready to do Europe yet."

"WHAT? You're not ready to do Europe? What does that even mean?" I was way past upset, way past shocked, and into dangerous territory.

"It means I don't want to spend *any* money to do a cruise to Europe."

With the last bit of patience I could muster, "If you didn't want to do this cruise at all, why in the fuck didn't you just lead with that? We have been going in circles about cost and now you just don't want to go?"

The entire disagreement was spinning out of control. We pumped the brakes before either of us said something we couldn't take back or worse, something that would escalate this to an entirely new level. We had both backed ourselves into our "points corner" and neither of us was interested in listening to the other.

It started out as a cost comparison. On the Bliss cruise we were in a smaller room that was more expensive than this potential transatlantic one. As further evidence, I broke down flying directly to Europe versus the boat to get there and fly back. Flights to Europe at this time were pushing around $2,000 round trip per ticket ($4,000 for both of us), then we would have a hotel for a least one week and of course ALL the food. Food alone would have been at least $1000 for the week. That's a ton of cash! The two-week cruise for both us plus one-way plane tickets home were under $3000

All my pitches on how economical this plan was didn't matter to him. I was willing to pay the money for a luxury experience. Having nice things makes me happy. All Lovie saw was dollar signs. Spoiler alert, we did end up booking the transatlantic cruise with a balcony several months later when deals were crazy good during the roll out of Covid. I also ended up agreeing to downgrade the Bliss room to an interior room as a bargaining chip. It was a $1,400 savings though, so I can't be too mad. Unfortunately, the pandemic was still in effect and our cruise was cancelled in 2021.

That one point I kept making, "it's worth the money to me," is where it got personal. You see, Lovie could live by himself in the woods. He could live out of his car and be completely content. He is not a material person, and he's frugal to a fault. To him, my desire for nice things can seem like a character flaw. That's right, a character flaw, like there is something wrong with me that needs to be fixed. I interpreted what he was saying in this conversation and naturally took it as a personal attack. He was judging me, telling me my opinion was wrong and unnecessary. That raised my blood pressure.

Our eyes were locked on each other, daring the other to say more. When there had been a long enough pause in this conversation from both of us, he stood up from his chair, walked across the room, and went to the bathroom. He was locked in the bathroom for couple minutes. I didn't ask if he was calming down or just handling his business.

When he came back out, any evidence of aggravation was wiped off his face. He wrapped me in his arms and laughed. "I have to laugh that our worst problem is what type of room to book on a cruise. Seriously first-world problems." And he is right. If this is the worst of it, I will take it. Just like that, it was over,

This conversation took me about two hours to really get over though. He had moved on in the amount of time it took to walk from the chair in our spacious state room to the bathroom, pee, and walk back over to the bed where I was sitting. I realized that I was as bothered by my reaction to this as I was to him insinuating I was spoiled, bad with money, and my opinion in general was wrong.

I totally expected him to just give in to what I wanted, no questions asked. He was putting up a fight about finances even after I said I'd pay, which usually settles everything. He knew I wanted this so badly and yet stood his ground and didn't cave right away. I was absolutely upset at the words he said and how he said them but I was partly mad at him because I didn't get my way. He goes out of his way to make all my dreams come true and this *one* time he pushes back, I throw a hissy fit? I had some internal work to do on this one- noted.

This is the reason I analyze all of our conversations and why it sometimes takes me longer to process. I need to understand where I can improve as a wife, a communicator, and as a human. I didn't give him time to process what he wanted in this situation and so he responded with "no" because he felt pressured. When a valid point was made, the other person was automatically on the defensive. We weren't in a place to be open because the pressure of a timeline (the lady was holding a room for us for that day only). In a way, it was like an ultimatum and ultimatums are never a good option for anyone. It is the fastest way to breed discontent, and no one ever wins.

So, if we don't fight about sex or woman, what is our most common argument about?

Tone. We, and by we, I mean me, are most often affected not by the meaning of the words or events that happen in our world, but by the tone in which certain things are said. Okay, maybe the tone in which things are interpreted. To reiterate, it's not what you say but how you say it. On the flip side of that token, you can only be responsible for the words you say. You are not responsible for what they hear. This is where egos need to be left behind. Leaving your ego means being able to recognize that no one has to be right or wrong. It's okay to apologize for how you worded something or apologize that you heard incorrectly. Arguments should lead to an understanding and focus on finding common ground, not proving you're right, and escalating to a fight.

Lovie is very direct and means what he says without needing to read between the lines. For some reason, this is often a problem for me. I am used to pleasantries and the concept of choosing your words carefully so as not to upset the person you are talking to. I beat around the bush. I hate confrontations. This is the opposite of how he communicates.

I have what we call girl brain. Girl brain is the ability to overanalyze a single sentence and find every potential, from death and tragedy to unicorns and fairy dust, without any actual details. Example: Lovie tells me that he's going to hang out with his ex: "Hello, my love. Going down to hang out with her." I think, *"They will say sweet words to each other, and he will fall for her again and then they will talk about getting back together. Then he might leave me."* I would then spend the better part of the evening thinking about crazy conversations that I fabricated and then craft my potential responses to him when he told me. This is all based on zero evidence or fact. I made every single bit up. The next morning, I ask how the night was, bracing for all the worst case. His response is "We hung out, smoked and then I came home around midnight." Literally stressed out for no reason.

This is not healthy or productive. Because every time we talked afterwards, the same response was given (I am paraphrasing here), "It was fun. No, we did not have any deep conversation. No, we didn't talk about getting back together. No, I don't want to get back with her."

Now here is the next part and might be the hardest one to do. You have to trust your partner's words—period. If you don't trust them or there is a history of dishonesty, there are many other things to work out before getting to this point. If you are poly, I recommend working through all of this before bringing in another partner, otherwise, it will most likely be a whirlwind of bad news bears. Having a third person will NOT improve your communication or trust if there is not a solid foundation already. I had to trust that the way he communicated events to me was true and correct for him. In this way, I am very lucky because he would say his highlights, answer every question, and his actions were not different from his words. She really was just someone to hang out with.

I wanted to explain girl brain in a somewhat extreme example so I can better illustrate the way my thought process works, and how we deal with the issues on tone. In all the time we've been together, I still haven't figured out how to take his directness. It always feels cold and a personal attack. I have learned over the years to be more assertive with my own voice and instead of assuming I know his intention, I ask what he means.

For many years he would say something that hurt my feelings and I'd walk away, internalize every word and create my own interpretations. This is a terrible idea. Now we had to two things to deal with. The original thing that started our disagreement and we also had to deal with my emotional analysis of the words he used. To be honest, it's not fair to myself because I waste precious energy on potentially nothing and it's not fair to him because he can't be responsible for what goes on in my head.

We're both committed to a life of happiness, love, and no drama. Because of this, we are willing to step out of comfort zones and ask for clarification on anything we don't understand or have questions about. This didn't happen overnight. It took years of work to feel safe when we feel very vulnerable. Depending on the conversation, the questions I ask for clarification will vary. For example, Lovie made a comment one day when we were discussing our upcoming Bliss Cruise that it would be way better if our friend Jasmine came with us. That was the comment, nothing more to it. However, I heard "If Jasmine comes with us, the cruise will be fun, otherwise it won't be as good." Obviously, that is not what he said, but I took the tone that he used and read into it. I had to follow up before getting moody and sad.

The questions I asked were: Are you saying it won't be fun if it is just us? Is there something else going on that made you say that? Clearly, typing this way after the fact and having a clear mindset, it's easy to see that all he was saying was that having her go with us would amplify the experience. Having that slightly uncomfortable conversation got us back to a co-hesive place without a disagreement. He is so unwaveringly patient with me.

Another example happened while we still owned the house with Pandora. For a year or so, there had been discussions on how to buy her out or have her buy us out. Hours of conver-sations happened between them, and she eventually agreed to sell it so everyone could move on. After I weighed pros and cons, we decided that I would- again- buy the house in my name, he would pay her, and be done with it. The home would now only belong to Lovie and me.

Keeping in mind that there are three sides to every sto-ry–yours, theirs, and the unbiased truth—I can only give my perspective on how things went down. Once Lovie and Pan-dora hashed out the details, her and I got on the phone and discussed the terms of selling. I was more than fair in what I offered. She agreed, and I thought that was the end of it. Oh no, it wasn't.

She then asked for an additional large sum from property that they had sold five years previously to pay off this current house and was now claiming she was owed "unrealized gains". This is the most absurd thing I've ever heard. I've heard Lovie yell twice in fourteen years, this was one of them. A feeling of hopeless just took over and we agreed to her ludicrous terms. It was the only way to cut that cancer from our lives.

While we digested the financial terms, discussion started on if we even wanted to buy at this point or just list it for profit to compensate for this unexpected curve ball. Tensions became high for several days. When I gave my opinion on how

I thought we should handle it, he shut me down. The tone he used made me think he was saying, "Your ideas are dumb and they make no sense." I had to defend myself and my point of view. I wasn't being treated as part of the team. The stress was pitting us against each other instead of uniting us.

This one did not get addressed right away; I needed more than the Five-Minute Rule to process. When I was ready to talk, I laid out how his words made me feel and what I thought he was insinuating. My goal in this conversation was to get him to understand why I took his tone as condescending and that I would like him to work on communication skills that were more compatible with mine. This conversation was frustrating for both of us because he is very stubborn and I can be too. Getting to where we both understood the other's point of view took some time, but we got there.

Notice that I didn't say we got to an agreement. That isn't always the goal. We got to the point that I understood his point of view and what he meant, and he saw where I was coming from. Mission accomplished. It helps tremendously that I have a partner who genuinely wants to make me happy and is willing to try different approaches.

Since we are talking about communication in relationships, *The Five Languages* by Gary Chapman is a must-read for understanding your partner's communication style. Knowing this has been a game changer in our life, especially in our triad. Everyone expresses love in different ways. The Five Love Languages are Physical Touch, Quality Time, Gift Giving/Receiving, Words of Affirmation, and Acts of Service.

When we first became a family, I wanted to shower Pandora with gifts. Gift Giving is my primary love language. When I buy a gift for someone to whom I want to show a lot of love, the price tag is irrelevant. This doesn't mean that smaller or inexpensive gifts mean any less or aren't important, they definitely are. On the flip side, when I receive gifts, I don't give any consideration to how much they spent. I am so thankful that the person thought of me, took the time to pick something out, and spent hard-earned money just so I would smile. The most meaningful gifts have a story behind them. Full disclosure, the only exception to that would be gifts from Lovie. I know he gave his unwavering commitment to me based on the price on my diamond ring.

The first gift I bought Pandora to show my love was a pair of diamond earrings. She told me she'd never owned real diamonds—bingo—the perfect gift from me to start our relationship. When I gave them to her, her closest friend questioned her why I spent that much money on a gift. Was I trying to buy her affection? Pandora questioned my motives. Of course, I was not trying to bribe her to be with me but from an outsider perspective, those who didn't know me or my love language, it could have appeared that way. Eventually, we learned each other's language and were able to know it was genuine.

Lovie's primary love languages are Acts of Service and Quality Time. It took me a while to put it all together. While I was giving him gifts and telling him "I love you," he was not doing the same for me. What he was doing was taking my car to put gas in it before I left for a work trip, calling the bank to handle something I needed fixed, researching things I didn't have time to do, and happily complying with any length honey-do list. He was chauffeuring me to run errands, just to be together. He traveled on work trips with me, canceled other plans when my schedule opened up, and always made our family date nights a priority. To this day, he still does all these things, willingly and with a huge smile, fourteen years later. Additionally, he has broadened the way he shows me his love by including words of affirmation, because he knows that is a big one for me. He doesn't need to constantly hear sweet sentiments to feel loved but has adapted how he communicates in a way that really resonates with me.

One of the greatest gifts Lovie gives me is his energy. Ninety-nine percent of the time we are in the same energy field and feeding off each other, which makes us stronger. The one percent that causes stress, helps us learn. During lifestyle events, whether it's at the club, on the cruise, a sexual experience, or with people in an individual setting, his vibration is higher. He is always focused on making sure we are connected, making eye contact, touching in one way or another, and asking how I am feeling. There is a genuine desire to share his extra energy with me and it brings us to a next-level love.

When we are interacting with other people, it is extremely important that we stay vigilant about what the other person is feeling. If there is ever a time that I don't like the situation or am not feeling the vibe, we have to walk away. No one should ever "take one for the team."

There are times when Lovie is enamored with a beautiful woman and misses my "subtle" signals. That's when I have to communicate more clearly. I'll ask him what's going on in his head, what is he thinking about, and this philosophy is carried over into playtime. Likewise, he will check in on me, do I feel okay, am I having fun. This is imperative in a poly/swinger relationship. It may feel awkward to ask during an experience or you may even be afraid of the answer you'll get. Never fear the response. If you're worried about resentment for being uncomfortable because they're having fun, you might want to have some hard conversations.

All relationships can be made or broken by communication. Choose your words kindly, come from a place of understanding and love and the number one rule to remember: it's never you against your partner, it's y'all against the world.

CHAPTER 15

REJECTION

Rejection sucks.

But, it is a part of life. We might get rejected for a credit card or not chosen for the job we have dreamed of. We know how to deal with this type of rejection. Physical rejection is more personal. It may be the one thing that can single-handedly cause years of hard work on self-esteem to be flushed down the drain. Seriously, I could spend three days mentally gearing up to go out, buy new outfits, take two hours getting ready, and, within fifteen seconds, feel like a troll if someone is uninterested in me. If someone ignores me, my feelings get very hurt and the rejection spiral starts. I run through ridiculous thoughts like, "I'm not good enough," or "I'm not pretty enough," or my go-to, "I'm too heavy."

There are people who won't be attracted to me, just like there are people I won't be interested in. I also have to remember that my husband has an amazingly strong presence in a room. It's hard not to notice him. It's hard for women not to be drawn into his charming and flirtatious vibe. He definitely has a way with words, and nothing feeds his ego more than a woman who has the "the eye of the tiger look," as he calls it. This means she is giving him a look that screams, I'm hungry for you. Attention towards him (or lack of attention on me) shouldn't threaten my self-esteem. I can still feel pretty without getting praise and being ignored does not negate my value, physically or emotionally.

There is one exception to this scenario. That's when Lovie and I are at an event and a female starts a conversation, oozing sexual attraction vibes toward him but does not even bother to say hello to me, just flirts with him. Then I don't feel like a troll. I just get bitchy. I mean, how hard is it to acknowledge the woman standing next to him? Saying hello doesn't mean you want to have sex with me; it means you are a nice human. Newbie tip: Always, always include the spouse of someone until you know their dynamic. You never know what their comfort level is, what their play style is, or what their relationship situation is. And, it's polite.

At this point in my life, I'm able to step back, process the way I feel, and move on. Yes, I may still feel some kind of way briefly. I'm a woman with big emotions. I'm not going to pretend like these things just roll off my back because that's not true. The truth is that my feelings get hurt if I feel rejected or I might feel insignificant for a moment. But I recognize that I have control over what I focus on. I have to decide to let those emotions go. What I don't do is allow myself to have a victim mentality.

Once we were in a group situation that I did not want to be in but I took one for the team. Lovie was in the mood to play and after a night of all drinking together, it was expected. (Which, by the way, is not a thing that should be normalized. Sex should never be expected. Get excited if you get laid, but if you don't, be grateful for the fun time and company; there's always next time.) I also was not physically attracted to the husband but was afraid of hurt feelings if I rejected him. It was my decision. I willingly engaged, I reinforced I was okay as everyone else was having fun and I allowed it to continue.

But I was not okay and I should have spoken up. This single event was a real turning point for me. I felt guilty for lying and uncomfortable because I knew I was faking enjoyment. The main thing I preach is be honest. Everything about this lifestyle is based on honesty. And I lied my way through that night. At one point, I actually had tears streaming down my face as I lay in bed during intercourse. I was done, and I didn't want to be there. Just in case there is any question in your mind, let me say this again: There was nothing inappropriate done by the other parties there, no one forced themselves on me, and everything was consensual. I was just done. I no longer was sexually attracted to the group, and I wanted to be lying in bed reading or writing, not having sex.

What should have happened, hours earlier, was having a conversation admitting I was not attracted to this couple and did not want to proceed. Giving a rejection can be just as hard as receiving one.

On our first Bliss cruise, we attended a seminar, and the speakers gave a brilliant way to communicate if they were interested in whomever they were interacting with. They had come up with this secret code beforehand in order to get a pulse on where the interest level was during a conversation. The husband would ask his wife if she wanted some red wine. If she said yes, that meant she was not interested and gave a segue for them to move on. If she said no, it was game on.

This is a subtle way to decide together if there is any interest. However, sometimes conversation is great and everyone is having fun, but a sexual connection is not there for one couple. Now what?

There's no need for a big event. No one wants a dramatic explanation. If, or when, sexual advances are made, just be direct. It is time to normalize saying, "Y'all are great and we enjoy hanging out, but we are not interested in playing." Of course, conversations don't actually happen that way, but the gist is there. It is okay to say no, do it in a respectful way.

This lifestyle has so many nuances that it can be hard to follow along. Just like any other clique, the circles are small.

Don't be that person who is rude or mean. Sometimes you don't even need to say the word no, you can just politely walk away and most people understand.

At the end of the day, we all want to feel loved and feel beautiful. Respect the differences in each relationship, speak kindly, and come from a place of patience with everyone.

The most important things: Love yourself in all your glory, put your partners before others, and work to make the world a better place.

Create your own paradise.

TO BE CONTINUED...

ACKNOWLEDGEMENTS

Some parts of my life have been "normal," some parts have been out there, and some things I still can't believe I allowed to happen. Through everything, I have received the love and support of the people who mean the most to me. I love each and every person who has remained by my side.

To Mom and Daddy, I know it's been different, but thank you for loving me as I am. I'm so blessed to have such an incredible model of love and partnership in y'all. We have had some growing pains together, but y'all never gave up on me. I hope you know how much I love you and will always need you.

To My Sissys, I love y'all. Thank you for being the laughter, support, and grounding I need.

To My Aunts, y'all are like moms to me. Thank you for the constant love and support.

To My Person, JR, you have been my rock through every single meaningful event of my life, even when you do not agree. You support my decisions and never fail to provide every point of view possible. We are on very different paths, but you have never made it seem any different. I can only guess what you have thought on the inside from my dilemmas. I would have never made it through everything without you. From the bottom of my heart, I know that without you, my life would have been way less authentic.

To Tiffy, we have had amazing times together. The way you always jump in for new adventures and try new things has inspired me. You've taught me so much about how to be myself, love myself, and not let anyone tell me what I should look like.

I am thankful you stuck with me for all these years. Distance, time, or life will never break the bond we have or the love I have for you. ( )

To My Boo, thank you for sharing life with me. I owe the next fifty years to you. Thank you for listening to every insecurity I have, every single time. Thank you for being my wingman during our most pivotal time. You taught me to take things less seriously, let things roll off my back, and how to be more patient. Every day you remind me to be optimistic and laugh. My love for you is eternal.

To My Lovie, I don't even know where to begin. Thank you for all the knowledge you have shown me. You have opened my world to so many different things. I love that you will do all the silly things with me, dress up together, match and color co-ordinate, and, most importantly, are willing to travel as much as I do (well almost as much) because you know it makes my heart happy. You have taught me about communication and the importance of being 100 percent honest. I know we can, and have, made it through anything. I loved you then, I love you now, I'll love you forever.

ABOUT ATMOSPHERE PRESS

Atmosphere Press is an independent, full-service publisher for excellent books in all genres and for all audiences. Learn more about what we do at atmospherepress.com.

We encourage you to check out some of Atmosphere's latest releases, which are available at Amazon.com and via order from your local bookstore:

Finding Us, by Kristin Rehkamp

The Ideological and Political System of Banselism, by Royard Halmonet Vantion (Ancheng Wang)

Unconditional: Loving and Losing an Addict, by Lizzy and Adam

Telling Tales and Sharing Secrets, by Jackie Collins, Diana Kinared, and Sally Showalter

Nursing Homes: A Missionary's Journey Through Heaven's Waiting Room, by Tim Eatman Ph.D.

Timeline of Stars, by Joe Adcock

A Boy Who Loved Me, by Wilson Semitti

The Injustice in Justice, by Charmaine Loverin

Living in the Gray, by Katie Weber

Living with Veracity, Dying with Dignity, by Alison Clay-Duboff

Noah's Rejects, by Rob Kagan

A lot of Questions (with no answers)?, by Jordan Neben

Cowboy from Prague: An Immigrant's Pursuit of the American Dream, by Charles Ota Heller

Sleeping Under the Bridge, by Melissa Baker

The Only Prayer I Ever Have to Say Is Thank You, by M. Kaya Hill

Amygdala Blue, by Paul Lomax

ABOUT THE AUTHOR

SARAH JOLICOEUR is a Corporate Coach with over 15 years of leadership experience. As a National Director of Training and Development, she helps develop and implement new coaching programs. She is a certified Executive and Life Coach. Sarah and her husband have been in the Poly and Swinging lifestyle for 14 years and she is moving her skillset into the Lifestyle arena. They currently have a farm in South Florida. This is her first book chronicling her personal journey into polyamory.